It's earlier 'tis getting

the Christmas book of
Irish Mammies

COLM O'REGAN

TRANSWORLD IRELAND

TRANSWORLD IRELAND
an imprint of The Random House Group Limited
20 Vauxhall Bridge Road, London SW1V 2SA
www.transworldbooks.co.uk

First published in 2014 by Transworld Ireland,
a division of Transworld Publishers

Design by Curious Design
Illustrations by Doug Ferris, Marie Dunne and Peter O'Sullivan

A CIP catalogue record for this book
is available from the British Library.

ISBN 9781848272071

Addresses for Random House Group Ltd companies outside the UK
can be found at: www.randomhouse.co.uk
The Random House Group Ltd Reg. No. 954009

The Random House Group Limited supports the Forest Stewardship Council®
(FSC®), the leading international forest-certification organisation. Our books
carrying the FSC label are printed on FSC®-certified paper. FSC is the only
forest-certification scheme supported by the leading environmental organisations,
including Greenpeace. Our paper procurement policy can be found at
www.randomhouse.co.uk/environment

Printed and bound in Great Britain by
Clays Ltd, Bungay, Suffolk

3 5 7 9 10 8 6 4

Contents

A (very brief) Few Words
from Mammy

Excuse me now, I'll be with you in a second. WILL YOU MIND WHERE YOU'RE GOING WITH THE TREE? You nearly had the Sacred Heart off the wall.

Anyway, where was I? Oh yes, Christmas. Well, as you can see it's all around me at the moment between lists and cards and IF A FEW PEOPLE GAVE A BIT MORE OF A HAND AROUND THE PLACE ... Oh look at them, as if butter wouldn't melt in their mou— which reminds me, I must get more butter for the ... anyway. I go. All. Out. For the Christmas, but that's just me. There's plenty of Mammies are far more sensible and take it in their stride. I was only talking to Sheila Carter the other day. Says I, 'Are you all set for the Christmas?' 'Oh Missus,' says she, 'I. Couldn't. Give. Two. Hoots. I don't let myself get stressed. I just let Himself take care of everything and I pick up what's left. There's no point in everyone being stressed.'

I envy her, I do. As you can see, 'tis all go here. And we've visitors as well. And would you believe, they have *dietary requirements*! In my day dietary requirements just meant you were hungry for your dinner. But shur anyway ...

We'll have a full house and I don't mind. It's good to have them. There's families missing people this time of year and it's tough.

Now if you'll excuse me I've a million and one things to be doing so I'll let the young lad tell the rest of it. He's better at the typing.

Mammy

Introduction

Mammy and Christmas — they go together like a stressed-out horse and carriage. In an Ireland where so much is changing, where so much is uncertain, Christmas* is something constant to hold on to. It promises peace, joy and goodwill even though it might still spit us out the other side, exhausted, cranky and swearing we're not going to TOUCH another Quality Street.

This book is just a glimpse into the multifaceted world of the Irish Christmas and where the Irish Mammy fits into all of this.

You'll meet different types of Mammies as they negotiate their way through the minefields of competitive Christmas Lights, the string of visitors, the trips up to town, the white-hot meat of Christmas Dinner; later, of course, quite a few Mammies have to deal with the quiet of January when 'They' are all gone back.

And hopefully you'll learn about some Irish traditions that make our mild, damp Christmases *a little bit unique*, such as:

---

* Or, to give it its proper title 'The Christmas'. As in 'Are you all set for The Christmas?' Or 'How did you get over The Christmas?'

6

- The DHRINK. We beat ourselves up over our dhrinking in Ireland but behind the headlines there is much nuance to how we enjoy ourselves. Except the Twelve Pubs. That's definitely binge drinking.

- The 8th of December – the official start of the country Christmas. Marking the day when country Mammies still venture up to Dublin to wait for two hours to get parking.

- Stephenses night – the social occasion of the year when you must return home to the town of your birth and be judged.

- The *Late Late Toy Show* – the time when the metaphorical Christmas lights of television are switched on and four-year-olds are allowed to stay up late. If you're one of the children fortunate enough to appear on it, it's the best way to make your mark on the TV-watching public's consciousness.

- The dos and don'ts of buying a goat as a charity gift and other buying guidelines.

We also welcome back some old favourites such as *Irish Mammy Magazine*. In 'The Christmas Edition' we join Mammy and Himself in their home as they prepare for 'the holiday season' (as Mammy never calls it).

Somewhere underneath the tinsel and stuffing, Christmas was of course originally a religious festival and the book explores all that that entails from the tense situation around choir practice for Christmas Eve mass (because the bishop'll be there and it's going out on the Internet) to how the Christmas story is re-enacted by all the little dotes in the primary school nativity play.

Speaking of which, finally we tell the greatest story that has never been told, the Christmas story of someone who has never been given a voice, who was excised from history – Joseph's Mammy.

So we begin our story of Christmas, not at the beginning but a little bit before it.

Colm O'Regan

I

Ghosts of Christmases Past

Of course in my day,
Christmas was very different.

Roman Holiday

Like most Christian feasts, Christmas has its origins deep in the pagan past. Although it was soon subsumed into the feast we recognize now, the mid-winter capers of our Roman and druidic forebears are still to be seen in how we celebrate today.

The Roman Empire was the origin of Saturnalia — a feast dedicated to the god Saturn that occurred around the time of the present-day Christmas holidays. Saturnalia was marked by a number of traditions that we continue today, most notably carolling and the giving of gifts. The gifts to children were often wax dolls. The dolls represented the humans whose lives had been offered up to appease the gods during the year; which, if you think about it, is Very Irish Mammy.

The Romans also celebrated *Dies Natalis Solis Invictus*, which means 'birthday of the undefeated sun'. There were many versions of this in Northern Europe as people celebrated the solstice. In Ireland this was marked as the Feast Of The Stretch In The Evenings – a rumbustious affair when villagers would cavort semi-naked and exchange whispered small talk about whether the days were getting longer or not. Archaeology has also unearthed some very early forms of Christmas decoration.

Within a few centuries, though, the Romans found their Invictus evicted and their Saturnalia slung out, because there was a new kid in town.

Mother of all Mothers-in-law

The Booker Prize shortlist always raises eyebrows and 2013 was no exception — not least because of the staggering omission of *That's More Of It Now: The Second Book Of Irish Mammies*, a decision born of pure jealousy, no doubt because *they* didn't think of writing it. That's the way with these judges. The other surprise was the brevity of one of the entries

— at a little over 100 pages long, *The Testament of Mary* by Colm Toibin was the slimmest-ever book to make the list. It's a reimagining of the life of Jesus' mother Mary and it prompted a welcome examination of life around that time.

But there is another story that has not been told. What about Joseph's Mammy? If she was alive at the time of the Nativity, there's no doubt she would have had her own cross to bear. But we didn't know anything about her. Until now. The discovery of an ancient papyrus scroll has changed all that. It appears to have been written as early as a couple of days after the Nativity by Joseph's Mammy herself, judging by the shopping list scribbled on the back of it.

MILK & HONEY

TEA-TOWELS

NUTS FOR PUSS

SPREAD

SLICED MANNA

SOMETHING FOR
THAT CHILD I SUPPOSE

Using these snippets, a truly unique historical account has been created. Here is an exclusive excerpt from the story of Eunice, mother-in-law of Mary.

And if this isn't nominated for the Booker, then the whole thing is a pure cod.

Excerpt 1: Talk

Eunice had a face on her. It was just one thing after another. And that boy of hers was responsible for most of the things that were following each other at the moment. Joseph sat fidgeting at the table, glancing up now and then from his food.

'Are you finished your olives?'

'Mammy ...'

'Because if you're not going to eat them I'll give them to the cat.'

'Mammy ... M-Mammy ...'

'Life goes on for Puss. She doesn't care about any news. Would you like a few olives, Puss?'

'Mammy, don't mind the cat. We need to talk about this.'

'What's there to talk about? How you got involved with that wan I don't know. If ye'd even have waited until ye were married ...'

'Mammy, it wasn't like that. It's a bit more complicated.'

'Complicated! It seems dead simple to me.'

'But Mammy ...'

'What your poor father lordamercyonim would say I don't know.'

Joseph almost told her the full truth but didn't think she was in the humour for understanding sacred mysteries and might just think that someone was making an eejit out of him. Eunice frowned but said nothing. He was a good lad despite it all and he'd done a lovely job with the shelves.

'Well, I suppose you'd better be off now. Have you some place to stay? You can't have that baby born in a stable somewhere.'

Excerpt 2: Inn Time

Joseph was sweating slightly as they stood in the doorway. The day had not gone well. Everywhere was full. His mother's words were ringing in his ears: 'Whatever you do, don't leave it too late.' Now they were in the last inn.

The innkeeper regarded them suspiciously. 'A room – for the two of you. Have ye booked?'

'No, it was all a bit last minute.'

'Right, I see. We're fairly full with the census. We have one little room over the tavern but it's quiz night tonight so it won't be ideal. You're welcome to give it a go anyway.'

'We'll take it.'

She glanced at Mary.

'And herself, has she long to go?'

'Well, I don't know, to tell you the truth. I'm a bit new to this ...'

'I see.'

Her tone suggested she saw a lot but this was the kind of carry-on that she especially disapproved of.

'And what name shall I put on it?'

Joseph told her and immediately saw the innkeeper raise an eyebrow at the different surnames.

'Oh, so is she keeping her own name? Very modern.'

Joseph grimaced at his mistake. He supposed they were married now. Were they? That's what the angel had said in the dream anyway. If it even was a dream. He'd have to stop eating cheese so late. The innkeeper made one last mutter of 'notions' under her breath and handed them a key.

'I'd suggest you get some sleep while you can. The quiz nights get fairly competitive around here. Especially the picture round. It's quite iconic.'

Excerpt 3: Labouring under a misapprehension

Six hours had passed. The noise from downstairs had not lessened. The quiz seemed to have stopped but now it looked like a band of Country 'n' Eastern musicians had started up. For the first time on this journey, Mary was cross.

'Joseph, this can't go on. Will you go down and tell them to whisht?'

He left. Mary listened as his voice came from below, earnest and pleading. The music stopped. As he returned, there was laughter and the music started up again. Except now the lyrics of the songs seemed to have been altered and directed at Joseph. But Mary couldn't worry about that now. By the time Joseph had returned he had bigger problems. She was walking around the room breathing heavily.

'I think the baby is on the way, Joseph.'

'How do you know?'

She looked at him. He understood.

'Right, "the angel said it". What do we do?'

They listened for a moment as the song 'Come out ye Nazarene bastards' filtered through the floor.

'I can't have him here, not with that going on.'

'How do you know it's going to be a b– sorry, OK, where is my head at today? Well, where do we go?'

'The stable? It'll be quiet. Can you run and get the innkeeper? She'll have to do as a midwife.'

They parted at the bottom of the stairs. Mary went to the shed. Joseph ran off to find the innkeeper. She was not happy at this further evidence of carry-on but was a practical woman and labour was labour so she went with him. When they both approached the byre, they could hear a baby crying. The innkeeper started running, shouting to Joseph over her shoulder to make himself useful and get some water. He was returning with the water when she intercepted him. The Face had returned.

'Are you trying to make an eejit out of me?'

'What do you mean?'

'Well, either that baby can walk through walls or she wasn't carrying him in the first place. I went in, all set to clean up, and there she is, cool as a cucumber, feeding the baby, not a drop of sweat on her. She was glowing in fact – GLOWING! No blood, no cord, not so much as a SIGN of a birth ... and ... who's THIS?'

They both watched as some shepherds walked past them towards the stable.

'It's a bleddy circus. I want ye out of here as soon as she's fit. I don't know what way ye do things in Nazareth but I never saw a labour like it.'

As she walked away Joseph thought she might be due a visit from an angel in a dream fairly soon. As predicted, the innkeeper was all smiles the following day. Hot crusty bread and cheese arrived and the finest of swaddling clothes. When the cattle came in for the evening, it looked like someone had been shining their hooves. Which was just as well, as some high-powered visitors arrived shortly after.

Excerpt 4: Sinai Trouble

Meanwhile, Joseph's Mammy Eunice was in a perpetual state of Nawful as she confessed to a friend.

'... and by the way, Jesus they're calling him.'

'Jesus? I never heard that name before.'

'I think it's some name from her side.'

'And where are they now?'

'Oh stop! I'm after getting this scroll now and he says in it – Don't get mad Mammy but an angel appeared to me in a dream and told me to go to Egypt as it wasn't safe for us here.'

'He's a divil for the angels.'

'That shaggin' angel! Rachael, God forgive me but if I got my hands on that angel I'd wring his neck for him. If it's a him. You wouldn't know with their "get-up". Disrupting all our lives. I don't know what's got into my boy.'

'Ah, he'll turn out alright. I'm sure there's some plan for him with Himself.'

'Well, I wish he'd tell me. Where's my angel telling me what's going on? What are the neighbours going to think about all of this? You may be sure they're talking.'

'I haven't heard anyone say anything. Maybe it'll die down.'

'I don't know. Miracles do happen, I suppose. As long as The Ancient Chronicle don't get wind of it.'

Unfortunately for Eunice, the local paper had more than got wind of it. No thanks to Joseph.

The Ancient **CHRONICLE**

NO COMMON CENSUS

Councillor fumes at Roman 'carry-on'

There were stormy scenes at Nazareth Urban District Council during the week as Michael Galli-Lae launched a strong attack on the census organized by the Roman Emperor.

A HAMES

'It's a hames,' he said. 'NO organization at all. Lads are going back to the place of their birth and there's no accommodation. I heard one story of a child being born in a stable.'

A Roman spokesman said that while he could not comment on individual cases, Herod was very interested in any story of a child being born in a stable and would urge the parents to get in contact so that they can receive whatever assistance is available.

LOCAL MAN MEETS KINGS

It was a case of 'Hello there, your Majesthree' over the holiday period as local man Joseph ben Heli from The Glebe, Nazareth, had a surprise encounter with three foreign Kings in a Bethlehem stable.

The Kings were visiting the area on unspecified business when they bumped into the local man in a stable on the edge of the town. Ben Heli was in Bethlehem for the census when he met the Royals.

'They were so down to earth, no airs or graces but you could tell they had a bit of star quality.'

It was a busy couple of weeks for the carpenter as he became a father. His 'wife' Mary gave birth *contd page 7*

Is your transport making an ass of you?

Use a horse of course.

The national and international press weren't far behind. Even here in Ireland, the story received very prominent attention from hitherto unheard-of ancestors of our current national newspapers.

Hibernian Independent

INSIDE: ROMANS CANCEL *ALL FIVE* INVASIONS. WHAT DOES THIS TELL US ABOUT IRELAND AS 'A GREAT PLACE TO INVADE'?

Ireland's Golden Couple cheer on the new arrival

Fashionista and recent new mum, Amy Huberhominus was among the first to congratulate the new parents Joseph and Mary on the arrival of their new Saviour Jesus. 'Sooo excited for the guys,' she said.

Hubby Brianus Driscollicus followed up minutes later.

'Obviously at the end of the day it's a big result for the family but also for humanity. Good stuff Mary and the Joester #bigday'

The baby boy Jesus was born in a star-studded ceremony in the rustic stable in one of Bethlehem's boho-chic up-and-coming areas.

It was a private ceremony attended by a few close shepherds and kings but the *Hibernian Independent* managed to get exclusive figurine carvings of the happy family. Dressed in a simple blue and white robe from the House of David complete with halo, Mary was radiant while partner Joseph sported a beard.

A friend told the *Hibernian Independent*: 'Obviously it was a surprise to the couple when they heard they were going to have a baby but they've been so amazing and the little tot is great. Even though He's the Saviour of the world He's been very normal about it. But just wait until He hits the temple and wedding circuit. Everyone says He's going to have a big impact.'

The new parents are set to take a quiet family holiday in an unspecified location – believed to be Egypt – away from media attention and the wrath of Herod.

PROPERTY
40-page crannóg supplement
Discover your lakeshore hide-away

FASHION
Cooley Brown Bulls
This season's 'to-die-for' accessory

THE HIBERNIAN TIMES

Trinity graduate boosts town with 'Census Sensibility' event

Some twenty thousand people are expected to descend on Bethlehem this weekend for an innovative new event, which it is hoped will provide a huge boost to the local economy.

'Census Sensibility – Don't Dare to Secede' is the latest brainchild of Trinity graduate Saoirse Herod who admits he's not a little nervous about how it's going to go.

'Basically the idea is that everyone registers their name and then just hangs out. It's the networking opportunity of the millennium.

'Anyone who's anyone in Galilee is here. People are mingling, there are huge synergies and all the attendees are astounded at the level of talent here. Some wonderful new army companies are being formed and everyone's wondering who will be the Next Big Thing, the next Messiah in this industry.'

The event is not without its critics particularly since it has quickly hoovered up all the accommodation in the town. There are reports that even the rooms in the maternity wards have been occupied.

Herod defends the impact of his event. 'We're all about disruption.'

The Hibernian Examiner

One of the shepherds 'may have been from West Cork'

S<small>THE</small>UNDAY BUSINESS SCROLL

Markets Hold Steady on News of Messiah

Mass Appeal

Christianity arrived in Ireland and gradually Christmas began to take on the shape that we recognize. Even though Christmas became cemented in the Irish calendar, it was not without trials. With the advent of the Penal Laws, the traditional Christmas Eve Mass was often held in straitened circumstances.

A Very Irish Christmas

At the turn of the 20th century, the Irish embarked on a campaign to redefine their national identity. This spanned nearly every aspect of Irish life and even Christmas was swept up in the front line as Irish organizations sought to convince the Irish to use their own native terminology and not to be still in thrall to Empire, as can be seen from these very strident Gaelic League posters of the time.

CHILDREN REMEMBER!

SANTY COMES TO IRELAND

'FATHER CHRISTMAS' COMES TO BRITAIN

MAKE SURE YOU'VE POSTED YOUR LETTER
TO THE RIGHT MAN!

Luckily, the Irish Christmas is no longer caught up in such questions of identity. In a more pluralist Ireland, there is a far more live-and-let-live attitude — we hope.

It's just as well, because with Christmas fast approaching, there isn't time to waste. Preparations are afoot!

2

Preparation Anxiety

Every year I tell myself I'm not going
to worry about Christmas.
And. Every. Year. I get into the same state.
All for one day.

Early Adopter

There is a particular type of Mammy who seeks to conquer time by trying to get ahead of it. The passing of one Christmas is merely a reminder to start worrying about next year's Christmas. She only experiences true relaxation for about an hour after the turkey is served and someone else is doing the washing up.

Unfortunately, such restlessness can unsettle other Mammies with whom she comes into contact. You might hear a conversation like this one sometime in June or July:

'Did you have a nice time in town, Mammy?'

'Ah! I did and I didn't.'

'What happened?'

'I was inside in Debenhams, you know, not getting anything, just browsing, because they know how to charge in there I can tell you ... anyway, you'll never guess who I met.'

'We've been through this, Mammy – I never guess so you might as well tell me straight away.'

'Aren't you very smart? Well, 'twas Cora Shouldice!'

'Remarkable.'

'No, but you see I don't know when I laid eyes on her last. And there she was, laden down with bags. "You must have won the Lotto," says I. Not that she'd tell me, mind. Those Shouldices are like the Cosa Nostra. Complete omerta.'

'We should call the Guards.'

'Are you going to listen to my story or make comments?'

'Go on, Mammy.'

'So I said to her about, you know, the bags and did she win the Lotto and the rest of it, and she said, "No, I'll let you into a little secret: Christmas," says she. "Christmas?" says I. Says she, "I do all my Christmas shopping this time of year and then I don't have A Thing to worry about when everyone else is stressed." Except now she has me stressed thinking about it. 'Magine! Christmas shopping in the middle of the

summer, if you could call it a summer.
"Look at this grand jumper I got for Paddy,"
says she and she showed me this top and that
top and ... anyway, I was worn out talking to
her, she was so well organized.'

'Well, if she's bought clothes for her family,
she's screwed if they want to return them.'

'Why is that?'

'Because the thirty days'll be up and the shop
won't take them back. So they'll be stuck with
them.'

'IS THAT A FACT? Now! So she isn't so
smart after all. I can't wait to tell her that
now. Just for her own information.'

'Just for her own information? But Mammy,
maybe don't do it just now. It'll look like you
were thinking about it too much.'

'No, you're right. I don't want to give her the
satisfaction.'

'And you don't want to get on the wrong side
of the Shouldices, especially if they're Cosa
Nostra.'

'What did I say about smartness?'

Meanwhile, Puss observes matters with the usual aloof tolerance of human weakness.

Ignorance was Bliss

Regardless of who you are, though, Christmas becomes impossible to ignore. Even Puss knows it's on the way. Despite a slight increase in treats, as far as Puss is concerned Christmas is a load of unnecessary fuss. The cat will keep an ear out for that fateful phrase:

In the midst of the helter-skelter, there are a few milestones.

- **The Christmas cards**: I don't know is there any POINT in sending them these days. I don't know does anyone read them … but they're nice to get all the same.

- **The decorations**: That tinsel? Would you believe, that tinsel is older than you.

- **The trip to town on the 8th of December**: I'm leaving at SIX whether you're ready or not. It's the only way I can be sure of parking.

- **The food**: You'd swear there was war coming with the queues.

Card Race

Eventually they will be doomed: the pack of thirty Christmas cards, bought to support the good work being done by the Poor Sisters of the Blessed Situation, the Daughters of Faith, Hope, Charity And Also The First Cousin Of The Woman Down The Road, or the They're Not Just For Christmas Unwanted Pot-Bellied Pigs Shelter.

Increasingly, people would rather send their messages for free through Facebook, so much so that the very currency of the Christmas greeting has become devalued. Curiously, at the same time, the concepts of privacy and sharing information have also become devalued, meaning that now people tell practical strangers information that would barely be hinted at in a private Christmas card.

We have gone from this:

To the Costigan Family
Happy Christmas to ye.
We are all fine here T.G.
Himself is over his little bit
of 'trouble' too.
Nuala Mick & the girls

to this ...

Whatshername Ithinkshesafriendofmycousin
Happy Christmas to all my peeps 2014 was a touhg yr wit all dat stuf wit Darren but tank God de skumbag is out of my lif and hope he and dat skank have a grate time NOT! Lol

Just want to say tanx for all de luv dis yr and also tat I kudent get trouogh it widdout the luv of the Angles. Evry1 has a gardian angle. U just hv to luk hard for it ...

Ciara Sexyface Hey hun hope ur ok. Kant wait 2 cu. Been 2 long. Will bring lots of wine LOL

Jonners J Angle haha ya fuppin eejit. Srsly tho happy x mas

Marie Cogan Hello pet will you give me a ring?

Whatshername Ithinkshesafriendofmycousin
LOL Jonners my spellig is atroshus tanx Ciars love YA. Will call u Mammy tmw

However, there are some stalwarts who will keep sending the cards until the end, for whom there is still excitement at getting the roll of Christmas stamps. Talk to a Mammy who has just finished writing and posting hers and you will encounter someone who has grabbed a few hours of serenity before the Christmas stress rises again. A good place to find her is down the post office in early December.

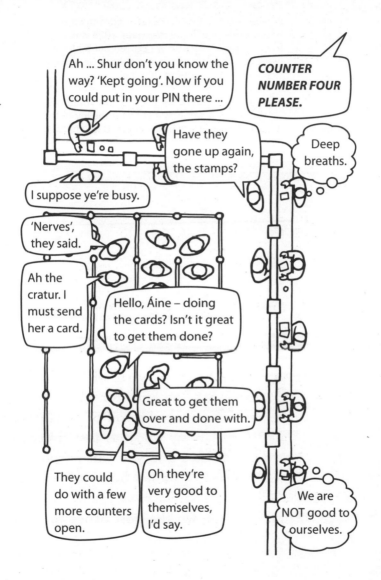

37

A diaspora situation altogether

'More cards. I hope now it isn't anyone who wasn't on my list …
Who's this? It's a photograph! Who would that be from?'

If Christmas cards are to go, one genre will be missed: the Christmas cards from America.

To all our Irish friends,

2014 was a great year for the O'Malley clan! Patrick-Joseph and Kathleen gave us little Baby Molly. She so much reminds me of poor Patty who passed this year. Colleen graduated high school and is taking Celtic Studies at Hatchatawnee University and she plans a semester in Ireland real soon. We are so looking forward to seeing you guys when we go to Europe next year. Much love and God's blessings to you all.

From Mary-Kate, Gerard-Anthony and all the O'Malleys – Erin, John Paul, Kevin, Brendan, Shawn, Cody, Daniel-Patrick, Caden, Donovan, Griffin, Quinn, Brianna, Megan, Colleen, Reagan, Bridget, Brenna and Baby Molly.

The faces of Irish America are interesting — like what would happen if Ireland stepped through a wormhole in space–time into an alternative universe where there had been no famine and we'd been colonized by a better-looking nation — maybe the Dutch. There's a certain skin and hair-tone typical of the Irish American. A lot of the men look like Jack Nicklaus or Mitt Romney. The women look like one of The Golden Girls.*

Newer greetings cards

As ever, the reaction of a certain proportion of the population to technology is to 'go artisan'. And why should Irish Mammies be excluded from this? It is now possible to submit your own designs. Online. Mammies can finally say exactly what they want when sending cards, with no need for reading between the lines.

---

* This may be the last generation of Irish people to look at the Irish American face with a certain awe. With a more multicultural population, the native Irish will hopefully soon receive a much-needed transfusion of genes from other countries. While good for our self-esteem, this will also probably lead to the demise of the Irish Face — the asymmetrical, irregular physiognomy that promised whimsy, the chance of mischief and not giving a straight answer because you wouldn't know who might be related. It's already evident that good nutrition and dental care is causing the Irish to have better bone structure and regular features, giving us the look of people who long ago would have been the types to eat a continental breakfast the morning after a wedding.

Deck the Halls ... but only if we've enough tinsel

Branching out

Artificial or real? The artificial tree is like owning a car, but without the depreciation. Although it has a higher initial outlay, it pays for itself after a few Christmases.

Buying a real tree every year, on the other hand, is like getting a taxi. It smells vaguely of pine, makes no sense financially, there are huge variations in quality and you may end up dealing with a series of gruff no-nonsense men wearing fleeces. Still, there is a great sense of ceremony about it.

You drive to the local tree centre, your excitement in stark contrast to the calmness of the man who sells it to you. He has seen many Christmases come and go. There's a fag clamped in his jaw as he listens impassively when you say you'd like a 'good tree'.

He gestures with his hand to where the trees stand like navvies waiting to be hired outside The Crown in Cricklewood.

'They're all good trees.'

They lean against the fence wrapped in netting. You try to gauge what they might look like unwrapped.

The most important thing to check is if the base is drilled straight. If not, the tree on the stand will list drunkenly.

The best way to stabilize a crooked tree is with a book, but be careful which book you choose. A hardback surface will be too resistant and the tree might slide off. Better to choose a paperback with a soft mushy interior so that the stand settles into it and gives greater stability.

Others will avoid this eventuality by cutting the tree themselves.

'Where's Daddy?'

'Gone to get the tree.'

'Where's he getting it?'

'He knows a fella.'

Himself knows a fella alright. Specifically, he knows a fella who grows trees and where there's a gap in the fence through which a resourceful type of Himself might get in with a bow-saw and take a tree. He only takes a tree that mightn't get noticed. He tells himself that he's providing a service by thinning the crop for the owner — albeit without telling him.

Last year, the tree was so miserable that Mammy wasn't a bit happy.

'We can't use that.'

'What's wrong with it?'

'Where's the rest of it? There's only branches on one side.'

'Well, it'll fit better in the corner so. You're always saying how hard it is to get the tinsel in around the back of it.'

'Why can't you just buy an artificial tree?'

'Are ya mad? The price of them!'

'We'd have an artificial bought with the money you spend on petrol going around scavenging like Bear Grylls.'

'There'll be no artificial tree going into this house.'

'I'll go out and buy the tree myself. That thing looks like something out of "Thriller".'

Himself had looked so hurt by this that it was as if she'd criticized his ability to start a fire. In the failing light he went out again with the bow-saw. His suggested solution later on that day was so ludicrous she could hardly object and she was laughing as she saw ...

'Two trees!'

'I stripped the branches off one side of it and it can go on the inside. Two bockety trees making one good tree. It'll be like a symbol of yourself and meself.'

'Speak for yerself. There's nothing bockety about me.'

But she couldn't object any further. She was very fond of him, even if he did act the gom.

'We'll have to get another angel so.'

Once the tree is up, it's time to put something on it.

Lights, Camera, Inaction

'How in the name of God do we have FIVE sets of lights and none of them working?'

Mammy has her suspicions. She clearly remembers telling A Certain Person to gently wrap the lights around a stick. Now stick and lights all lie forgotten in an old A-Wear bag, an orgy of different sets twined around each other like those mating snakes you'd see on a wildlife documentary – except with no spark between them.

It's a common problem. Decorations are put away on grim January days when no one is in the mood for dwelling on the sheer non-Christmasness of the situation. With the soundtrack of 'That Hoor Of An East Wind' whistling down the chimney, they are just stuffed away with all the other decorations. Everyone just wants to get on with surviving the first weeks of the New Year.

Then in mid-December, after a bit of crouched searching in the attic, under the stairs or at the back of Mammy's wardrobe next to the Mills and Boons, the decorations are retrieved, along with a dusty old extension cable. The lights are plugged in.

And then someone has to go and get new ones.

Decorating the tree is a job that is not handed out lightly. It requires skill and an eye for colour. Small children will often produce the most avant garde creations as they are unencumbered by height.

Once established, a house's Christmas traditions can be very tenacious. The jobs that each person does around Christmas are more permanent than any other job they have for the rest of their lives. Any attempt to change that order of things is met with resistance.

'I'm doing the tree.'

'I want to do it this year. You always do the tree.'

'Because I'm the eldest. I was doing the tree when you were still wetting the bed.'

'But I want a go.'

'You're not qualified.'

'What kind of qualifications do you need to decorate a tree?'

'I did Engineering; you only did Arts.'

'Stop that, the pair of ye. I'll just get Donie to do it.'

'He's seventeen – what would HE know about it?'

The decorations themselves are equally tenacious. Many of them survive from when the home was first set up, along with the good bone-handled knives and some sheets lost in the hot-press. Once you have enough to do a respectable job, the ones you have will do you grand. There will always be some attrition: a child's experiment a few years ago to see whether tinsel burned in different colours; the bag of baubles that got loose in June and ended up inexplicably in the hedge; two shepherds from the crib who joined a group of plastic zoo animals and were last seen with leopards blu-tacked to their shoulders.

There have been additions too: the cardboard angel with the terrifying smile that the first child made in Senior Infants, which can't be thrown out because it's an important relic of that time; the garish overly-large silver reindeer that was a present from a neighbour and has to be visible when they call, as they always do, on the 27th. Otherwise, decorations are a memento of the home in its early stages.

Even the bags they are stored in can be small historical fragments in themselves, with supermarkets' old branding, like Dunnes Stores colours before they went all 'modern' or Quinnsworth ('Remember your man Maurice Pratt who used to do the ads? Whatever happened him?'). Or they can be the only surviving remnant of a department store in 'the town' that has long since shut down. Taking them out again reminds Mammy of when you got your first school trousers there and the 'grand family' that used to run it until 'the son went off the rails with drink and the horses' and it was sold for flats.

And so the Christmas decoration ceremony ebbed and flowed in a relatively steady state for years. Then, as the last century drew to a close, the Irish discovered the room outside. After years of watching American Christmas movies, the Irish started taking things to the next level. Christmas lights crept out of the sitting room, up the stairs and then out the windows and doors like some sort of electric ivy. At first it was tentative. The daughter would venture outside to throw a few lights over the small tree in the front garden. But within a few years, Himself would be up on the roof with the ladder with a cable clip in his mouth and a hammer in hand, swearing as he battered the fascia in order to string up lights along the roof.

They showed some restraint though – unlike the crowd next door …

Even for those Mammies who eschew much of the Christmas fuss, the world around soon reminds them what time of the year it is.

3

The Signs are There

Halloween not even over and they've started
showing the toys on the telly.

It All Ads Up

For a brand, it is the Promised Land: when your advertisement enters the national discussion and twenty years later is still there. Some ads can officially launch the start of a season. Any ad for Kerrygold showing sultry foreigners and flighty locals throwing shapes around the butter is usually a signal for the single population to go out and find a mate. Similarly, commercials for Kellogg's and the ESB kick off Christmas in Ireland.

The Kellogg's ad shows three children planning to stay up to watch Santa arrive. They leave out cornflakes for Santa and hide behind the couch to wait. But it is the hero of put-upon youngests everywhere who seals the deal when she meets the big S.

This was one of the television moments that made Irish people build houses with 100-foot sitting rooms when they grew up. In the pivotal scene she totters towards Santa and is still walking a few seconds later, apparently unhindered by a wall. All of us wanted that house. But they cost a fortune to heat. And where were the parents while their children fell asleep behind the couch? Out at some charity ball no doubt, like the ones they had in America.

That ad couldn't have been set in Ireland. Mammy would have been in like a shot.

The other perennial ad is for the ESB. The Mammy waits at home for the young lad to be collected from the station by his father. He is back from Dublin; you could tell from his haircut and good coat. Mammy is smiling beatifically as she takes care of the electric blanket, brown bread and a casserole. They embrace at the door. It's timeless. Although since deregulation, the ESB wouldn't quite have it all their own way now.

There is one recent entrant to the Christmas ad canon. The Bóthar Goat has entered the brain through the classic trick of repetition.

Charity presents are an antidote to the waste that can go on at Christmas gift-giving time. Be careful though. Make sure that you are confident your gift will be well received. It may be prudent to have a back-up present ready underneath the cushion. Watch the recipient's face carefully and gauge the reply. If the goat was for Mammy, you'll know you've made the right choice if you get a hug and hear this:

> 'A GOAT! We were just talking the other night about how we can make a real difference in such an unequal world. Thanks so much. Actually, it's a bit of a relief to get it because I was worried what you'd say when I gave you this beehive.'

However, you're in trouble if it's more like this:

> 'A. Goat. I see. Great imagination gone into that. The presents that you can get these days … A goat, if you don't mind … So, I suppose I'd better start peeling the spuds now. Right, let ye clear up this wrapping paper.'

At that point you should whip out the back-up present and say, 'But I got you this as well for yourself.' And there is relieved laughter all round.

The return of these ads is one of the stimuli that kickstarts 'the Christmas'. From then on, the urge to do the first big trip Up To Town starts to build. But timing is everything.

Town and Country

'Madness it is. Pure. Madness. I had to come out of the place.'

'What time are we leaving tomorrow morning, Mammy?'

'We're leaving at six o'clock in the morning – not a minute later.'

'SIX, Mammy?! You know it's Dublin, Ireland we're going to – not Dublin, Ohio?'

'I want to be sure to get parking. There'll be a ferocious crowd up from the country.'

'What'll we be doing all morning, Mammy? Nothing will be open.'

'Well, you could come to Mass with me.'

…

'The look she gives me!'

The 8th of December: It's not quite what it used to be. Traditionally it marked the day the plain people of Ireland made an expedition to Dublin for the Christmas. It is the feast of the Immaculate Conception – one of a number of feasts in the Catholic calendar that children just took as read without asking too many questions about what it meant. In the grubby, earthly sense, it meant a day off school and going 'up to town'.

In preceding decades, the influx of Your Good Jumper and Dingos jeans, accompanied by cries of 'Hold Mammy's hand VERY TIGHT, DO YOU HEAR ME?' were noticeable on the streets of Dublin, as were a number of other phenomena:

- Honking of horns as those unfamiliar with the streets became paralysed by indecision and the apparent unwillingness of Dublin drivers to give them any leeway. 'CAN'T HE HAVE A BIT OF PATIENCE? ... I'M TRYING TO ... THIS BLOODY "ONE-WAY" ... WHISHT BACK THERE WHILE I'M ... NO, YOU CAN'T HAVE TAYTO ... Thank you ... at least there's one dacent man in this ... AH I'M GONE WRONG AGAIN!!!'

- Idiosyncratic parking as people couldn't fathom what was so wrong with 'just shticking her outside Clery's'.

- People asking for snack boxes in McDonald's and Burger King.

The importance of the 8th of December has diminished in recent years. A combination of buying online, the presence of big shopping centres on the edges of most Irish towns, and modern consumer habits which see it as Christmas every day, mean that one particular day is no longer the be-all and end-all.

Despite this, many will still take the Christmas trip up to town and the 8th of December is as good a day as any. But, the queues. The queues were only. Out. The. Door.

Mammy found one place reasonably accessible.

Or you could take public transport. For the older country Mammy this means doing that thing they're always telling their children not to do: taking out their purse on a Dublin street.

Luas change

Mammy stands at the machine and speaks indirectly to it.

> 'Now where am I going? Arnotts, I suppose … That's zone 1, Press the … Why won't it press the bloody yoke?'

The likelihood that the touch-screen on a Luas ticket machine will freeze is directly proportional to the size of the queue behind you. Mammy looks at her finger to see whether she can spot some sort of malfunction. She hears a voice at her shoulder.

> 'Are ye alrigh' dere, missus?'

Mammy presses the destination a bit more hurriedly. This fella is definitely outside her comfort zone but she can hear the passive aggressive sighing in the queue behind her so she needs all the help she can get.

> 'Oh it's this fecking thing. It's not working.'

> 'It's de gloves, missus. It won't work with de gloves. Where do you want to go?'

Mammy tells him. She could have made up her destination but in Dublin on the 8th of December Mammies are only really going to one or two particular stops. A strong expert hand reaches over and starts tapping the screen. She notices weather–

beaten skin, some Indian ink on the arm with some names and a sword with a snake.

The screen beeps as it co-operates. It's as if the machine and the man have reached an understanding during the long hours he's spent leaning on it.

'Aren't you great now?'

'Ah not bad, missus. I've the Midas touch, wha'? Terrible cold, isn't it?'

'Oh it is, but 'tis dry I suppose.'

'Dry, dat's de main ting. Ye can put in yer munny dere now, missus.'

'Oh yes … two euro thirty … let's see …'

Mammy fumbles in her purse. This is it now, she thinks. She can already hear herself the following afternoon on the phone to Joe Duffy.

'And was there much in the purse, Yvonne?'

'Ah, you know Joe. I'm 78 and a widow, Joe. I didn't have much in it, just a few bob, but it's all I had for the presents.'

'I know, yes, yes, gowan. And tell me, Yvonne, did you get a look at his face?'

'I might have Joe but you know … you don't think about that at the time.'

'Where was he from? Was he Irish?'

'Oh yeah, Irish, Joe. Talked a bit like yourself, you know, Dublin. But anyway, I put in my money.'

'And this chap, as you say, was he alone or do you think he had an accomplice?'

'PLEASE TAKE YOUR TICKET AND YOUR CHANGE' says the machine, the lights flashing underneath. It might as well have been winking at its partner.

'Oh, the change, where do I get that?'

'It's just down dere, missus.'

'There in the little chute. I see it.'

'You have to see the change before you can be the change, wha'? And missus, if—'

'There-you-go-now-that's-all-I-have-thanks-very-much-bye-now-bye-now. Happy Christmas to you bybybybe.'

'—you had any to spare, you see I haven't eaten in … oh t-tanks very … much. Happy Christmas to ya.'

Mammy walks purposefully along the platform, urging the tram to come quickly as if it were the last helicopter out of Saigon. The unofficial Luas ticket assistant stares after her, puzzled.

Later, on the Luas, she has time to mull over the incident.

The Luas stops. Mammy gets out. Time to get to work. The window shopping isn't what it used to be, however.

Switz-swoo

Most Irish people have a well-defined list of things that aren't the same any more. This list includes attention spans, the size of a Chomp, and a relaxed attitude to Health and Safety.

Every winter, the list is topped by Christmas shop windows.

One of the must-do tasks on the classic 8th of December trip was the Switzers shop window. The very darkness of the morning, and the length of the journey — passing through the midlands town that was a handy place to go to the toilet, then the suburbs that looked like a scene from *The Commitments* — made it all the more magical when you got there.

City children took it in their stride. They might be back tomorrow. But country cousins drank in the sights of street lights, the choirs, the cartons of cigarettes hidden under the wrapping paper. And then there it was: the toy factory in Switzers window. They pressed their faces against the window, desperately wanting to join the fun inside.

I wish they wouldn't press their faces against the window.

I know. It's kind of distracting when you're operating machinery.

Even polar bears were put to work. This was before Global Warming so it was possible to look at polar bears without hearing David Attenborough's voice in your head intoning:

> *'But how long will these proud creatures, who have graced this planet for 20 million years, be able to make toys undisturbed by human activity?'*

While dolled-up Christmas windows still remain, no one does Santa's workshop quite like Switzers any more.

Back to the present day, it's time to visit the Living Crib* – to get some acting tips.

Going Nativity

'Some bit of a sheet'll do you I suppose.'

Let's take a moment to salute the primary school teachers. They have to tread a tricky line between the expectations of the parents, the constraints of the education system and of course the reality of the children themselves.

---

* A specially constructed stable scene at the Mansion House in Dublin containing actual cows, donkeys and sheep. It is a magical place for children and also for a few Himselves who do a bit of leaning and wondering where they got the grand straw.

Around this time of year, they will put themselves forward to be scriptwriter, costume designer, director and producer as the school puts on the Christmas concert or the Nativity play.

Due to the lack of actual contemporaneous visual evidence of what life was like around the year dot, we can only guess at the clothing worn by the main protagonists in the story of the Nativity. Based on the evidence of most Nativity plays, this included various types of bed linen tied with belts and head-dresses made from tea towels (the third-best tea towels).

Deciding who gets what part is a delicate task — not necessarily for the children but for the teachers and the parents. Certain ambitious Mammies may take umbrage at what they see as the lack of good roles for a girl (their girl) in modern theatre.

'And who's playing the Virgin Mary? Who? Of course she is … They were never shy about putting themselves forward, the Tolans. I'll bet Geraldine had something to do with that now.'

The truth is often more prosaic. For the younger children, the doling out of plum roles is usually done on the basis of which children are most likely to remember any lines at all or least likely to wander off stage in the middle of the show. Messers might be handed less crucial roles like 'the chorus', the back of a donkey or an extra shepherd. The donkey will provide light relief intentionally through its appearance or unintentionally when rumour goes around the rest of the cast that the front half – played by the chief messer – has farted.

'JACK CORRIGAN, DO THAT ONCE MORE AND I'LL PUT YOU WANDERING IN THE DESERT WITH NO STABLE TO GO TO, DO YOU HEAR ME NOW?'

The Nativity play will roughly stick to the accepted version of events as described by the various Gospels although some teachers will use the script to make a point at the expense of the current government. This will hopefully get a laugh from the audience.

Narrator: 'Den the Rome-ins said every one who is from the land of Isray-ill must go to reg … regis … register in their home town.'

Joseph: 'It's just one ting after another. First the septic tank charge, now this. We should get our union to look into this, not that it would make much difference.'

A titter from the audience acknowledges the out-of-the-mouths-of-babes moment, while noting that the New Teacher is 'fairly active' in that kind of thing.

More often than not, it's the ad libs which will have the biggest impact.

Shepherd 4 *[raises hand]*: 'Miss? Canigotoilet?'

For the Nativity play to triumph, hard work and dedication are required. The primary school teacher exhibits the classic Mammy traits: management, planning, conflict resolution and weary good humour.

An event like this allows Irish grandmammies to see just how much school has changed since they were younger Mammies. As well as interactive whiteboards and computers in every class, the older Mammies can also see how the pupils have changed.

'You were missed at the senior citizens do yesterday.'

'Well, do you know where I was? At young Emily's Christmas play.'

'Aaaahh.'

'The DOTES!'

'Is that the programme?'

The Local School Presents

The Christmas Play

3rd and 4th class Ms. Grimes

Narrator - Sarah Traynor-Tolan
Mary – Precious Martins
Joseph – Sean Moraru
Innkeeper – Sean Breen
Shepherds - Conor Twomey, Ella Cogan,
Tiernan Tierney, Lucy Healy
Kings – Afshin Tehrani (Melchior),
Haresh Kutty (Caspar) Ahmed Jaber (Balthasar)
Chorus – Emily Houghton, Derry Gilhooley,
Ben Shaughnessy, Saoirse Thomas
Angel – Gabriel Okonkwo
News reporter – Jack Deegan
Enda Kenny – Bogdan Crowley

'The names! I remember there was a fella in my class who got picked on because his name was Gordon.'

'And the children don't bat an eyelid. Anne Marie was saying that Emily wants to go to Abuja on her holidays to stay with Precious.'

'Abuja? I hadn't been any further than Abbeyfeale when I was that age.'

'And it was the most historically accurate play I'd ever seen. All the wise men were from the right places and all.'

'Apart from Enda Kenny.'

'Yeah, I think they put him in there to make a point, but the little boy playing him forgot his lines.'

'Ahh, the cratur. Did you get any nice photos?'

'Couldn't get near the front. There was such a crush, I was afraid I'd be knocked over and put out the new hip.'

The red carpet paparazzi ain't got nothing on a group of parents trying to photograph their children on any kind of stage.

Some children have a Christmas performance on a much bigger stage.

ToyZone

'There'll be no one let stay up for the Toy Show if ye don't stop messing. Now get into your pyjamas while the ads are on.'

The Late Late Toy Show is among the most watched television programmes in Ireland every year. It's not unlike *Willy Wonka*: a middle-aged man allows children to run riot in a place that has seen better days. But nothing bad happens to them — they just get to play with toys.

Watching it is a tradition. Small children are allowed to stay up to an ungodly hour, a new frontier of lateness, all huddled together on the sofa like a litter of excitable pups.

The *Toy Show* is *The Late Late Show's* finest hour. It's probably the only night of the year when normally easily enraged viewers are placated. There have been three *Toy Show* presenters:

· **Gay Byrne**, who gets the credit for everything. All GB-era *Late Late Shows* are golden because there was nothing else to watch at the time. No one can remember the dull ones and they're not on YouTube. Gay Byrne also benefited from having grey hair when he was presenting in his later years. It's much easier to affect good-humoured puzzlement when you have grey hair.

- **Pat Kenny**'s most celebrated *Toy Show* moment was The Tearing Up Of The Tickets. A winner in the postal quiz was offered tickets to the *Toy Show* but refused and Pat tore them up in chagrin. The jury is still out on whether this was the right thing to do and If Gay Would Have Done It. If Gay had torn up the tickets, of course it would have been the right thing. It's much easier to do good-humoured ticket-tearing when you've grey hair.

- **Ryan Tubridy** has had the toughest job wearing the *Late Late Show* mantle. His reign has coincided with the recession, the advent of social media as a means of watching television, the decline in patience and the resultant 140% increase in rage among the population. And his hair isn't grey enough yet.

But then the *Toy Show* comes along and all is forgiven. It is Ryan's finest hour where he can dress up and act the eejit, there isn't a soap star in sight, the audience is interested and no one knows who the guests are but no one cares.

Presenters have changed but mainly it's about the children and the toys. The toys themselves can cause some awkward moments in houses.

These risks aside, it's an enjoyable way to watch the different types of children we all once were. There are a few:

The child who says nothing with the toy that doesn't work

Kids don't always say the funniest things. Often they say nothing. The presenter has to assume that he will end up providing most of the answers himself.

'And what's this you're playing with?'

[whisper]

'Is it good?'

'Yeah.'

'And what class are you in?'

'Fourth.'

'And who's your teacher?'

'Ms Goulding.'

'Is she nice?'

'Yeah.'

'So you like this toy.'

'Yeah.'

'How does it work?'

[no answer]

'You're not releasing a statement at this stage.'

[Audience laughs, her Mammy in the Green Room is an odd mix of pride and mortification. The young one was all talk in rehearsals.]

'I turn this switch, do I?'

'Yeah.'

'And then what happens?'

'Then you press this here.'

'I press this, do I?'

[no answer]

'You'll make a great politician someday.'

[Audience laughs again. Ryan presses the button. And nothing happens.]

It is important that at least one of the toys doesn't work at all. It's good for children to learn that toys break when they are not looked after. When they don't work, there is disappointment and disappointment is good for you. With any luck the child may snap out of their daze for a punchline.

'You didn't do it right.'

The quirky boy with the unusual interest

Dressed in a dicky-bow with hair side-parted like in *The Little Rascals*, this is a child who is already destined for a big future. A combination of doting hipster parents, the requisite weirdness that every well-adjusted ten-year-old should have and a refreshing lack of self-awareness make him a viral hit. Watch out a decade later as he turns up again as a millionaire having sold his tech company FishSpoon to venture capitalists.

These children are not to be confused with:

The talented child

These are the Billie Barry kids of this world. She is in stage school and has a big smile as she does the thing from *Annie* or the other thing from *Frozen*. Her Mammy is just off the side watching and mouthing the words with her, wincing ever so slightly at the tiny slips. Over time, her daughter may lose interest in all of this but the VHS/DVD/YouTube will still be there as a reminder to Mammy of the time when it was the most important thing in the world.

The cute child

These children are usually fascinated by farming and deeply engrossed in telling Ryan how to attach a toy slurry spreader to a tractor. For cuteness overload, the producers will show the secret recording of the 'smallies' brought in to play before the show started. No performing for the cameras, just cherubic expressions, but always in the background you should be able to spot one of the children assiduously breaking a toy or crashing a tricycle into a cameraman's foot.

At home, Mammy turns around to look at her brood, trying to figure out which group they fall into. There doesn't seem to be any sign of TV in them yet. Although there is drama. Too many Pringles too late has brought on a dose of the runs. Mammy sighs. Billie Barry will have to wait.

But enough about the children for the time being; won't someone think of the adults? Luckily, there are a number of pre-Christmas events that appeal to an adult's inner child. And adults' inner children like to take a drink every now and then.

4

Drink Taken

I suppose they'll all be OUT of it tonight now.

Twelve Daze

'TWELVE PUBS! The Lord Save Us.'

The Irish are to drinking what Apple's New Products Department are to computers: always coming up with a new way to do much the same thing you were doing before, only more of it and faster.

One of our innovations has become, in a very short time, a Christmas tradition — albeit one that has not gained universal approval. Although it does have ancient forebears*, the modern twelve pubs started around the beginning of the millennium when we suddenly discovered we had money. As a nation we cast off a lot of Mammy's advice like an unloved anorak. Mammy would say too much of a good thing is a bad thing. Instead we thought, too much of a good thing means there is just more of the good thing than there would have been if there had only been enough of a good thing. How could that be a bad thing?

---

* The twelve pubs may have originated with the Anglo-Saxon tradition of wassailing. This was where groups of revellers went from tavern to tavern annoying everyone else with an exaggerated sense of group identity and wearing naff animal skins in an ironic way.

Initially the twelve pubs was a great way to avoid getting stuck for the whole night talking to a knob who had a habit of saying things like: 'Seriously though, derivatives is where it's at, man. All the top goys are in there.'

The age-group has got younger and now seventeen- and eighteen-year-olds can be seen cantering around like bullocks escaped from a town mart. And in the best traditions of Irish attitudes to alcohol, the biggest problem is that these youngsters *can't handle their drink.*

When a twelve pubs group bowls into an otherwise quiet pub, everyone tenses up. Staff wear expressions so unfriendly it looks like shutters have just come down on their faces. The incumbent drinkers move their drinks to the centre of each table to reduce the risk of spillage as the herd rumbles through.

Not that anyone would say anything aloud. Overt criticism of the twelve pubs is a delicate matter, lest one be accused of being 'no craic'. To be 'no craic' or 'no craic at all' — or the sarcastic form 'oh he's great craic' — is a terrible affliction.

Mammy regards the tradition with horror. Thanks to increasing coverage every year, Mammy has added the twelve pubs to the list of things that Young People Get Up To which she Heard Them Talking About On The Radio.

This list includes:

- Swedish House Mafia or any concert requiring a Garda emergency response plan

- Threesomes

- Magaluf

- Prinking

- Tactical voms.

She can draw some small comfort from the fact that it's the one night of the year when she can be sure her child won't be COMPLETELY FROZEN on the night out. Whatever you might say about the motives for wearing an ironic jumper, at least there's some bit of heat in it.

Mammy isn't always at home fretting. Many Mammies can party with the best of them — especially the Office Mammies.

Party Politics

'Promise me now you'll behave yourself.
You wouldn't know who'd be watching.'

Mammyness is an eminently transferable skill and some Mammies will mammy more than just their children.

There are women ranging in age from early twenties up to retirement who, whether or not they have children of their own, are the vital social glue of a happy office. In addition to doing their jobs with seemingly effortless efficiency, they take a benign interest in the lives of others. They are the ones who get the cards and cake for the going-off-to-get-marrieds, the having-a-babies, the leaving-to-go-travellings.

You could leave that kind of job to the men but few men have the same thoughtfulness, preferring to mark special occasions with a playful puck on the shoulder and calling the person a bollix.

Office Mammy will often be involved in organizing the Christmas Party, including sending the invitations.

To:	COMPANY.ALL
Cc:	THE BOSS; HR
Subject:	CHRISTMAS PARTY!

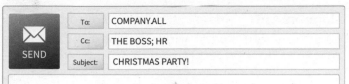

Let the madness begin!

The Sports and Social Committee is delighted to invite you to the
CHRISTMAS PARTAE!

At the
DONNEGAN ARMS HOTEL
Friday December 12th

FIZZY WINE RECEPTION
we're coming up in the world Vinnie hah?!

FOUR COURSE MEAL
with plenty of spuds, and a good dose of meat not like that swanky
place a few years ago.

AFTER DINNER COMEDY WITH
The fella off the telly, you know him, it'd be on RTE2, late.

AND MUSIC FROM
The band that did Eimear's wedding, ah they're very good. Banjos and
a trumpet, the whole shebang. Yer man the lead singer is a PURE
character. He had us all up dancing and poor Karen did her ankle.

DISCO
DJ Seamus P (resident DJ at Club Mystique, Ballybrunt)

RSVP by Monday week
and not four minutes before the bleddy thing is about to start.

There will inevitably be a mixed response around
the office.

Like many big occasions, the best part of the office Christmas party is arguably the earlier part of the day at work that precedes it. There are approximately two productive hours before the organization loses its tenuous grip on discipline and descends into a loosely connected procession of buying breakfast rolls for 'soakage', sitting on the edges of desks discussing where to have the pre-pints and replaying some highlights from last year's festivities.

It's like the last day of primary school before the holidays when you were allowed to bring in your toys. Except instead of toys you bring in your hopes and dreams for the night ahead.

Most of the women will be on a half-day to get the hair done. The office smartarse will interrupt a conversation about dresses with his own well-placed zinger: 'I'll probably wear a lacy black number meself.'

Some parties move seamlessly from work to the venue, but that can be a recipe for disaster. It's a well-known fact that 'The One That's One Too Many' (from the 'take it handy lads' anti-binge-drinking advertisement) is not consumed at the end of the night. A 'messy one' is far more likely if you drink 'The Four That Are Four Too Many' at the very start of the night.

The more sensible approach is to go home to get changed. This is where the other Mammies in this saga come in: the Mammies of the employees who still live at home. Their role is to repeat the following mantra over and over again while their offspring get ready to go out:

- Don't make a show of yourself.

- Don't make a show of yourself. Promise me.

- Don't make a show of yourself. Like last year.

Arriving back at the venue, there will be squeals as women who parted only two hours before greet each other again in their transformed states.

> 'Omigod your dress is GORGEOUS.'

> 'Oh stop! I'm bate into it. YOUR dress is FABULOUS. That's really your colour.'

Men nudge each other and say things like:

> 'A tie, Franky? Hah? Are you the solicitor or the defendant? HAH?'

Office Mammies play a few roles throughout the night. The first is to get up on the dancefloor 'for a bit of a boogie' long before anyone else has the confidence to do so.

> 'Pat, c'mon up with me, will you? This young crowd are too worried about looking cool.'

It doesn't matter if the music isn't very good. Years of encouraging children through tin-whistle lessons and attempts at artwork have trained them to show enthusiasm even when not enthused.

As the night goes on a number of interweaving stories reach their denouement and Office Mammy is often there to provide stability. A budding office romance – or rather an office romance taking place only in the head of one of the protagonists – of course comes to nothing. Turns out Jess has a BOYFRIEND and what's worse, he works for Concern in Malawi so he can't even be hated. All the time the jiltee wasted on dreaming up the possibilities. He moves on.

Perhaps now might be a good time to chat to Office Mammy with lines like 'Isn't this a great night altogether?' and 'Look at PJ out on the dancefloor – he's a real John Travolta!' With any luck Office Mammy might ask the jiltee if he has 'his eye on anyone'. The whole story will come flooding out and Office Mammy will tell him that 'that girl was a bit up herself anyway' and that 'there's plenty more fish in the sea'.

Indeed, in the hour he's been barking up the wrong tree he may not have noticed that the tone of the party has changed. When a large group of people all start drinking around the same time, they will simultaneously reach a tipping point. The room changes from 'merry and good natured' to a vista which resembles the orgy scene in the film *The*

Ten Commandments. People are twerking – including Dancing Mammy. Away in the darkness, on the dinner chairs, murky shifting has commenced as some of the other fish in the sea start to find each other. Spouses are having a right old go at middle managers about why there's been no pay rise even though their spouse is working ALL HOURS.

Another Office Mammy with the unenviable task of controlling the bar tab watches with alarm as the JobBridge intern exacts revenge for three months of photocopying by carting away trays of foul-smelling, flaming spirits. She tries to get the attention of the bar staff to shut it down, but they pretend not to see her for as long as possible, preferring to serve someone fifteen Coors Lights first.

The dancefloor is now full. The bosses who fancy themselves as being 'a bit of craic' are swaying awkwardly like the audience members who used to dance on *Top of the Pops*. You don't get where they are by being good at dancing. Except when Journey's 'Don't Stop Believing' comes on and the air-mikes and air-guitars are whipped out of nowhere.

Round about this time, the office 'quiet fella' (AKA 'Alltalk') will suddenly appear on the edge of the dancefloor. He has been filling awkward silences by hoovering up pints and is now 'in great form altogether'. He announces his arrival by sliding across the dancefloor on his knees to the chorus of 'More than a Feeling'. The whooping and cheering he receives goad him into ever-more ambitious moves over the next ten minutes: Hammertime, the Macarena, a moonwalk that is just him staring in one spot and standing on his toes and that breakdancing move where you hop around on one leg while holding the other. The last one will be the bridge too far for Alltalk and will topple him headfirst into the groin of the boss, who is sitting near the edge of the floor. She takes it all in good spirits but has mentally placed his name on a list of People She Might Not Put In Front Of A Client.

As the night reaches a climax, some Mammies, particularly of younger children, will check in with the babysitter, regardless of what is going on in the background.

By this time of the night, Office Mammy is dealing with the consequences of tantrums not only at home, but right here at the party. With the stress of the build-up to the night, there will inevitably be at least one meltdown. There is no one better at dealing with the aftermath of when Tired and Emotional and The Drink have combined potently.

The music stops. Office Mammy has had enough and it's time to go home. Others end up staying out too long. Way too long. This hardcore group style themselves as 'Legends', though their legendary status comes from being able to drink all night rather than fighting dragons or multi-headed dogs. They say things like 'What happens in Vegas stays in Vegas', but then spill all the beans at the first opportunity.

Inevitably, for these diehards, there will be a morning of regrets at home.

Speaking of home ...

5

Homing Instincts

What time will I expect ye? Oh not till then ...

Customs and Excitement

The airport at Christmas is a special place. There are choirs, criers — and, of course, correspondents. Everyone is sharing everyone else's homecoming. The cameras are trained on the doors out of Arrivals. But not everyone will make the news that night.

The journalists are looking for the most tear-inducing stories: a small boy carrying a 'Welcome Home Daddy' banner; a baby being dandled; groups of girls who are likely to scream. There is a gameshow-like tension. Who is going to be next through the door? With any luck there might be a few digs at the government thrown in as well.

A reporter goes up to one group who are swamped in balloons and banners that say 'RETURN OF THE MAC! Shaz McNamara Homecoming Committee'.

'And who are you waiting for?'

'My daughter, Sharon. She's coming back from Dubai.'

'And what does she do out there?'

'Nursing.'

'And could she not find work here?'

'Oh, the way the nurses are treated here is a bloody disAAAAH, THERE SHE IS!! SHARON!!!!!'

The doors have opened to reveal a small Irish bundle of a girl — with a great colour on her — pushing four times her own body weight in suitcases. The Fella She Got Talking To On The Plane slips away sheepishly thinking he might look her up on Facebook later. She is soon enveloped in a scrum of 'The Girls' — siblings, friends, Mammy and a toddling niece. An eleven-year-old brother who hasn't cried since the time the county were heavily beaten in the All Ireland, stands around the edge of the group smiling shyly, biting his lip, every so often swept into the ruck of the hug by a stray arm. Himself leans in, patting heads.

Inevitably the toddler will fall over a stray bag and cry because toddlers know instinctively when the centre of attention has shifted away from them.

> 'Ah, the poor girleen, too much excitement. Up all morning. Couldn't sleep last night. You can have your Tayto now.'

> 'Hasn't she got so BIG since I saw her last!'

> 'What do you think of your Auntie Sharon?'

> 'WaaaaahhIHURTMYKNEEEWAAH!'

> 'Overtired, I'd say.'

Groups hug their way towards the car-park, Mammy clutching her newly arrived daughter almost violently every ten paces. Himself is swept away too but has the presence of mind as he puts the ticket in the machine to briefly curse the prices.

So much talk.

> 'How was the flight?'

> 'Slept most of the way — big night last night. I came straight from the pub.'

> 'No change there anyway. Who was yer man?'

> 'A fella on the plane that I got talking to.'

> 'Jaysus, you never miss an opportunity.'

'Shurrup you, Daddy, haha.'

'Where did you get the grand coat?'

'In Forever 21 in the Dubai Mall.'

'Oh, would they have that out there?'

'The Dubai is the largest mall in the world, Mammy. They have everything. Honestly, you should come out, I keep saying it.'

'Well, we'll get you home first and no more talk of Dubai.'

Not everyone is this demonstrative. Others are awkward and shy. They wouldn't make a fuss if Garth Brooks himself came through and made a beeline for them, guitar and all, saying he'd just do the three gigs. A quiet engineering-type lad walks solidly out through the door. His Mammy and Himself hardly say a word but are just brimming with joy. This Himself takes hold of ALL the bags immediately. Better to keep the hands occupied or there'd be too much hugging, and then you wouldn't be able to hold it all in. There'll just be some conversation about the FIERCE traffic on the way into the airport, you must be tired and the room is aired and the electric blanket is on and you can get STRAIGHT into bed if you want to.

Arrivals is a beautiful panorama of excitement in all its shapes and forms.

Meanwhile, in departures, a lone Filipina is going home to see her family for the first time in three years. She's just as excited.

No Direction Home

Not everyone gets to go home for Christmas. Many households are facing the prospect of an empty place at the table as the Outnaustralias cannot always be there. Often the news is broken a few months earlier in a rather glum Skype call.

'Any word yet on what you're doing for Christmas?'

'I won't be able to make it, Mammy. I couldn't get the time off.'

'Oh …'

'I know, Mammy. But I'll definitely be home in March.'

'And you know Orla Deegan from the club was only talking to me the other day and she's organizing the Emigrants against the Locals match on Stephenses Day and she just wanted to see if you were around to get an idea of numbers. I said I'd ask you … but shur there's no point now.'

'I know, Mammy.'

'And you would have had your photo in the paper and the whole lot. So how did you run out of holidays, is there any harm in asking? I thought ye got plenty of days off.'

'I used a lot of them up to go to the Great Barrier Reef.'

'The Great Barrier Reef … But shur that'll always be there. I won't be around forever, you know.'

'Sorry, Mammy. Look, I'll be home in March. I'm going for promotion because I'll have a better chance of getting residency here.'

'RESIDENCY! IN THE NAME OF GOD ARE YOU TRYING TO KILL YOUR MOTHER BEFORE CHRISTMAS?'

'No, Mammy, you don't understand …'

'You talk to him, Daddy. I can't even look at him.'

'What kind of an eejit are yah to be upsetting your mother? They haven't taught you cop-on out there anyway I see. And I'm the one will get it in the neck now when you're gone. Great Barrier Grief, more like it.'

So now, on Christmas Day, there's a space at the table. Mammy has symbolically placed the iPad on the placemat.

'You're such a drama queen, Mammy. We're not in a reality TV show.'

'Don't tell me what we are or what we're not. Your brother is going to be here for Christmas dinner one way or the other. Now get the Skype going for me there one of ye.'

[*Brrrrrrut Brrrrut.*]

'Is it ringing?'

'It is, Mammy.'

'Hello.'

'Who's that? That's not Brian.'

'It's Lorcan.'

'Where's Brian?'

'Oh, he told me to say he won't be around for a couple of hours.'

'HE WHAT?! Where's he gone?'

'I think he might be at the beach.'

'THE BEACH! DOES THAT BOY GO OUT OF HIS WAY TO …'

'Or he might be behind you …'

'BEHIND ME … OH JESUS MARY AND J—'

'Hello, Mammy. Happy Christmas.'

[Everyone else] 'HAHAHAHAHAHA.'

If now is the era of Secretly Recording Mammy Getting Annoyed At Her Children, it is also the era of Recording Mammy Reacting To Surprise Homecomings. If you thought Mammy had language for the former, wait till you hear her in this mode.

If the Mountain won't come to Mammy ...

But sometimes they're not joking. There is no surprise homecoming. Sometimes, Mammy has to take matters into her own hands.

Having watched her brothers and sisters go away one by one thirty years ago, she's now had to help pack her own brood off. Folded their GAA jerseys that they'll wear on the beaches of Australia. Reposted letter after letter from the bank to them. So now, Mammy is Going Out To Them.

She told The Boy a few months ago:

> 'Well, I'm coming out to you. I didn't go through thousands of miles of driving you to matches and Feises and grinds to spend my time waiting for you to put a photo up on Facebook. Do you hear me now? Ready or not, here I come, as the fella said in the song. Let you be having a look around for hotels for me and Daddy.'

> 'OK, Mammy.'

Himself makes a half-hearted attempt to inject a bit of realism.

> 'It'll be an expensive Christmas this year.'

'Well, so what. For once I don't care about the money. We'll find it somewhere. I'm fed up of being at home listening to news about fights in Australia and what's going on in those mining towns and the whole lot. And we might as well have a holiday.'

And now she's here. In Perth. They went on a wine tour the day before Christmas Eve – A WINE TOUR! She's been smelling hints of burnt oak all day and Himself made a great show of swilling a slurp of lager around in his mouth. The young lad seems relieved as well, relaxed and tanned, miles away from Kalgoorlie where, not too long ago, there had been A Bit Of An Incident.

Of course Himself has been waiting a lifetime for the opportunity to do the one thing you do when you go to Australia for Christmas.

Your Place or Mine?

'Oh, I see. So this'll be the first Christmas I won't have ye all around. We'll have to make do I suppose.'

Not every homecoming is dramatic because of the distances involved. For some, it's about the politics. There comes a time in every relationship where one partner has to go to the other's parents' house for Christmas. Which set of parents to choose can be a fraught decision.

Imagine a coalition of two equal parties. Ideologically they are not too dissimilar though their supporters could come from different backgrounds. The coalition has to decide whether to pick one course of action or the other on a contentious issue. The grassroots hold differing views. Even a compromise may leave one side disappointed. You would not envy either of the party leaders having to stand up at the Ard Fheis and say:

> 'But we'll be over on Stephenses Day … or the 27th at the absolute latest.'

But how to decide? There are many factors that need to be taken into account. That's why it's best to take the scientific approach.

$$B_{mammy_n} = \frac{t_w A_h P(S_G) G^{a_p}}{E_{SR} C_s P(H_R)}$$

where:

B_{mammy_n} = Calculated benefit of going to a particular Mammy's house

a_p = Average age of parents

A_h = Area of parents' house

E_{SR} = Expected sleeping arrangements measured in number of rooms you will be sleeping in

t_w = Thickness of the walls between guest room and parents' room

G = Gravitational Pull (aka guilt) exerted by Mammy

C_s = Number of other siblings who will be home so it'll be grand if we don't go

$P(S_G)$ = Probability that other siblings will go on and on about how Mammy was disappointed you weren't there

$P(H_R)$ = Probability that Himself will be ranting during Christmas dinner about how most of 'them lads' are claiming the dole and working and this is a great country we live in isn't it?

When a Child is Born

Mammy is anxiously watching the road. The first grandchild is visiting for Christmas.

There is the sound of a car in telltale low gear.

> 'OH. THIS IS THEM! Quick, get up, Daddy. Ah, why are you wearing that oul jumper? I thought I told you to wear the nice red one I bought you. Go up and change now.'

Some hurried wardrobe readjustment is required. Meanwhile the new family are slowly extracting themselves from the car. The new father attentively opens and closes doors, buckles, zips, latches and fiddles with what seems like a system of ropes and pulleys. Hands calloused from holding shovels and hurleys and pints now carry a soft padded baby-bag with a picture of a cupcake on the side of it and 'Yummy Mummy' embroidered in pink thread. Then the new mother emerges with a cloth-wrapped bundle.

> 'AH WOULD YA LOOOOOOOOOOOOK. C'MIN, C'MIN, C'MIN out of the cold.'

Mammy presses an almost ferocious kiss on the new mother's cheek, as if she is trying to transfer

.mmy files by Bluetooth. Then, Himself hugs the new mother and pauses briefly before an awkward hug with the new father. Himself is adjusting to a world of increased hugging. At one stage he thought the man in the lawnmower repair place was going to hug him when he offered to pay cash but he must have been imagining it.

As the baby utters her first roar in her grandparents' house, Himself thrusts his hands deep in the pockets of his second-best trousers (the ones for wearing in the house when visitors arrive). He idly fiddles with a bunch of keys in case anything needs to be unlocked. But metal doesn't do a blind bit of good for this kind of scream, a sound that hasn't been heard around the house in quite a while, like the howl of wolves reintroduced into a National Park during a rewilding programme. Himself reaches into his special store of General Lighthearted Himself Comments.

'Nothing wrong with the lungs anyway, ha?'

Mammy is exploring the world of Mammies These Days.

'And have ye no buggy?'

'It's at home, Mammy, I use a sling.'

'A SLING! I thought that was your scarf.'

'It just goes over the shoulder and then through this ring. It's called baby-wearing. They say it's much better for bonding with the baby.'

'Isn't it lovely? Where did I see one of those before? I think it was in one of those brochures from Concern.'

The daughter raises an eyebrow in the direction of her own Himself.

'Yes, Mammy. Or maybe I told you about twenty times about them.'

'And how's the feeding going? You're feeding her yourself. Aren't you a great girl?'

'I'm giving it a go anyway, Mammy. I'd hope not to have to use the formula.'

'Deedn' it didn't do ye a bit of harm.'

'Was there much traffic on the road?'

This last interruption is from Himself. The son-in-law also senses that now would be a good time to talk about roads.

'No, there's a grand road there now.'

'Oh, mighty — they've it all bypassed.'

There follows a discussion about how long it used

to take to get through one famous bottleneck until the new species howls again about her introduction to a new habitat.

> 'I think she needs a feed. Is it OK if I …'

> 'Don't mind us now. You carry on, good girl yourself.'

Himself shuffles off to the window to look at the visitors' car, with a view to asking questions about its welfare and miles to the gallon. It will still be a while before all the Himselves of this world get used to natural processes like this.

Mammy thinks briefly back to her early days of motherhood and the various words of advice she got from the nurses about 'not to bother your barney' about breastfeeding.

> 'All the INFORMATION that's going now! When I had you shur I. Hadn't. A. Clue. It's a wonder at all ye turned out so well.'

The Krakow was Mighty

Aside from sitting on the wrong chair (see 'Places, Everyone') the first visit of a potential in-law to an Irish house can be a momentous occasion. Doing so at Christmas creates even more tension. It's like making your senior debut in the All Ireland Final; the sense of occasion places a lot of pressure to perform. And for the time being at least, a new element has been added to the mix: the visit to an Irish house of a Foreign In-Law.

'This is him now. YOU *[pointing at Himself]* be on your best behaviour.'

'Shur I'm always on my best behaviour. *[Himself looks out the window]* He's a smaller fella than I thought. The Polish fellas I knew were Tanks of Men.'

'Will you whisht …
HELLOHOWAREYEATALL?'

'Mammy, this is Cosmin.'

'How do you do, Cosmin? This is Himself.'

'Cosmin — that's a mighty name.'

'… Haha …' *[Cosmin laughs appreciatively]*

'What do you do for a living, Cosmin?'

'I work in IT, Mr Fennelly.'

'Mr Fennelly, hah! The only fella that calls me that is the bank manager. George'll do fine. But I thought Maria said you were in building?'

'Building websites, Daddy! Sorry, hun, Daddy thinks every Polish man works in building.'

'Mighty men to work — you should see the fella that was here a few years ago working on the extension. He was out to here.' *[Himself spreads his arms about six inches from his own sides to indicate the size.]* 'And it was all muscle. Well, he picked up a joist with one hand. I nearly had a heart attack looking at him.'

'Lukáš was Czech, Daddy.'

'I thought he was Polish. Shur I was asking him about Krakow and the whole lot.'

'He was too polite to correct you.'

'And he was telling me he used to eat FOUR BOILED EGGS for breakfast. Low GI, he says to me. Would you be a man for a big breakfast, Cosmin?'

'Yes, but no eggs for me. I am vegan.'

'VEGAN!'

Cosmin and Maria look at each other. They had hoped to broach this subject a little more gently. They hadn't foreseen a conversation about eggs while still standing on the doorstep. But they had underestimated Himself's worship of Lukáš Nemec.

Himself is about to launch into another anecdote about how a Hungarian fella was *a fierce tasty man to do a tiling job* and no doubt, as far as Himself knew, he wasn't a vegan when Mammy intervenes.

'Well, vegan or no vegan, we'll all be getting a cold standing here on the doorstep.'

She's not worried. She had been briefed earlier. Mammy is ready for anything once she has 'a bit of notice'.

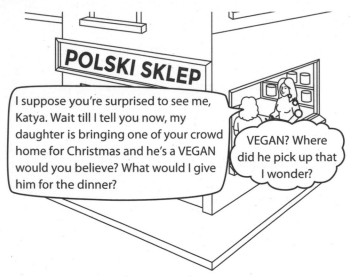

Wherever they came from, whatever age they are, they are children and once inside the door, the old familial relationships are re-established. In other words, everyone starts driving each other just a little bit mad after a while.

6

Didn't Age a Bit

Get UP! I've jobs for you today.

The house is full. Doors are opened and closed with more regularity than in a long time, letting in fierce draughts. There is noise and distraction. Personalities that haven't occupied this confined space for a while are brushing against each other. Adult children find themselves in a house-share with other adults but they didn't get to interview them for the room. For the most part, these brushes will be harmonious and in the correct direction. Occasionally, though, two of the siblings will come at each from the wrong angle and someone will get rubbed up the wrong way, like the top of a cat's head. And while we're on the subject of Puss ...

Sour Puss

Puss's whiskers twitch. The rise in excitement and tension in the house is palpable. Mammy is flustering around saying, 'I'll have to disturb you now, Puss' and 'Don't get too comfortable there, Puss, they'll be here soon'. The dog doesn't care but the dog is an eejit and also doesn't have to suffer the calumnies that Puss will endure. Pusses up and down the country are being disturbed from their 24/7 reveries by people who, unfathomably, can't leave a sleeping Puss lie. Where small children are present, Pusses have to use all their ingenuity to hide from twisted role-playing games.

Nor is Puss safe from older offspring. Mammy is from a more civilized age which understood a cat's role in the house — namely, to suit itself. (There is some ancillary obligation to provide companionship but it's generally understood that Puss's companionship is provided when it suits Puss.) Now cats are expected to sing — or at least pose — for their supper, to be cute for a living, to have humorous captions superimposed on images of them, to generate likes, shares, retweets and follows. So, when the house fills up again, Puss is forced to deal with the consequences of having an expressive face.

Puss realizes though that there is no point in judging the visitors too harshly because the biggest problem with people is that they are human. Humans are very susceptible to their environment. When the environment is the house they grew up in, humans of all ages can get a bit restless. It's the kind of thing that can give Mammy nightmares.

Driving Each Other around the Bend

But what really has Mammy's heart in her mouth is that she knows some of her returned offspring will want to use the car.

> 'I'm off to Clodagh's. Can I take the car?'

> 'OUR CAR! Oh, I don't know. I think you go a bit too fast. Remember you clipped the pillar? I'll drive if you don't mind.'

> 'Mammy, I clipped the pillar ten years ago when I was learning.'

There is no statute of limitations when it comes to Mammy and the car but still she tries another line of defence.

> 'Anyway, the roads might be icy.'

> 'It's thirteen degrees.'

> 'But there could be frost from last night – I saw snow up on the mountains.'

> 'But we're not driving in the mountains. C'mon, Mammy! I've been driving for four years in London.'

'This isn't London — you don't know what you'd meet around a corner.'

Eventually Mammy relents but more is to come — once they start the actual journey.

'We always come out FIERCE SLOWLY around that corner. OK left OK OK OK HOLD IT.'

'Ah, Mammy, I would have made that.'

'Shur what's the hurry on you? If you'd left in time …'

'I would have left in time if you weren't hiding the keys.'

'I was NOT. You must have moved them with your tidying. I had them in a Safe Place.'

After five minutes without her worst fears being realized and everyone ending up in the ditch, Mammy relaxes a little and takes in the countryside as a passenger, noting the important details.

'SALE AGREED, 'magine that. That place has been FOR SALE since I don't know when.'

'Where is SALE AGREED?'

'A house back there. You keep your eyes on the road. Mind this fella on the bicycle now.'

'I am minding him.'

'Mind … Mind … MindMindMind MIND.'

'HE'S FINE, MAMMY! WILL YOU RELAX? You're gripping that door handle, making me nervous.'

'You always were a nervous driver.'

Younger Every Day

There's something about the Christmas holidays that can make adult children briefly change into younger versions of themselves. They might have spent the rest of the year helping their clients to realize their potential using cutting-edge technology, leveraging human capital to garner greater market share, driving innovation, efficiencies and lorries, but once they slump into the old sofa, the years fall away.

Maybe it's the fact that Mammy has stored up Mammying for a few months and bombards them with attention and praise and sit-down-there-you-must-be-tired that renders some people helpless. Or it could be the house itself. Once back in those familiar surroundings, the scene of a thousand childhood squabbles, tiny old grievances are brought closer to the surface. Throw in a bit of bad weather-enforced close confinement and some drink, and high achievers who spend the rest of the year positioning their Fortune 500 companies at the heart of global change start regressing noticeably.

'Did you borrow my top?'

'What? Oh yeah, sorry. Meant to ask you.'

'C'MON, I WANTED TO WEAR THAT.'

'You can still wear it.'

'BUT THAT WAS THE ONE I WANTED TO WEAR. AND YOU'VE WORN IT OUT ALREADY. WHAT IF PEOPLE SEE IT?'

'Why are you getting so upset about this?'

'BECAUSE YOU'RE ALWAYS TAKING MY CLOTHES AND I WANTED TO WEAR IT AND NOW IT'S … OH IT DOESN'T MATTER.'

'Are you … are you crying?'

'It's just that … sometimes I feel like …'

'What? You feel like what? Seriously, Karen, I'll never borrow another top if it's so emotional for you!'

'DON'T PATRONIZE ME! YOU ALWAYS PATRONIZE ME. And you used all my shampoo and the hot water. You're so selfish!'

Mammy may have to intervene at this point.

'I'm going to town tomorrow. We'll get the shampoo and you can go looking for a new top then. And maybe both of ye might take it handy on the wine.'

If it isn't the tops, it's where to put the bottoms.

Places, Everyone

No one can remember just why you picked it or who picked it for you, but the place where you sat at your dinner table as a child will stay with you longer than most other constants in your life. It is a blueprint, part of the map of the house ingrained in your mind along with locks that need a bit of jiggling, crooked carpet bits that are hidden under chairs and the metal thing in the press that puzzled you for years until you found out it was your great-grandfather's Jew's harp.

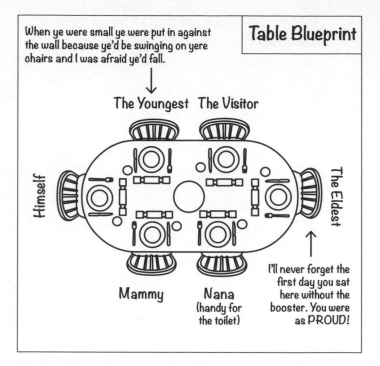

Table Blueprint

When ye were small ye were put in against the wall because ye'd be swinging on yere chairs and I was afraid ye'd fall.

The Youngest   The Visitor

Himself

The Eldest

Mammy   Nana
               (handy for
               the toilet)

I'll never forget the first day you sat here without the booster. You were as PROUD!

As families grow and disperse, the old blueprint can grow dusty, but eventually there comes a Christmas when the full complement of children sits down at the same time. Brief standoffs occur as two siblings go to sit in the same chair until a decades-old tradition asserts itself as the older sibling claims their rightful throne.

Himself and Mammy's place is sacrosanct — although there is a small percentage of Mammies who will eschew a place and just buzz around the table armed with condiments.

'Will you sit down, Mammy? We're grand. Your own dinner'll be gone cold.'

'Ah, I'm grand. I'm not that hungry. I'm just doing the gravy.'

'Mammy, sit down, I'll make the gravy.'

'You mightn't know how to work that cooker.'

'Mammy, I'm a mechanical engineer. I think I'll figure it out.'

[Pause followed by swearing]

'Mammy! How do you switch this thing on? It's the most un-user-friendly type of a—'

'I'll do it. You sit down. You'll be tired after all your engineering.'

A further complication to seating arrangements is added when the first potential in-law arrives for Christmas dinner. If you are spending your first Christmas with future in-laws, one of the top three questions you should ask in advance is: 'Where does your father sit?' The other two are: 'Should I call your mam by her first name?' and 'Do you think it would be OK if I took a bath?'

On the off-chance you've forgotten to do your research and are now faced with a table and are unsure of where to sit, here are some clues to help you avoid sitting in the wrong place.

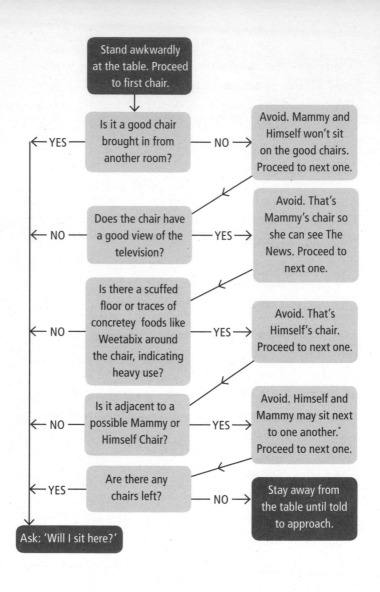

Stand awkwardly at the table. Proceed to first chair.

Is it a good chair brought in from another room? — NO → Avoid. Mammy and Himself won't sit on the good chairs. Proceed to next one.

YES ←

Does the chair have a good view of the television? — YES → Avoid. That's Mammy's chair so she can see The News. Proceed to next one.

NO ←

Is there a scuffed floor or traces of concretey foods like Weetabix around the chair, indicating heavy use? — YES → Avoid. That's Himself's chair. Proceed to next one.

NO ←

Is it adjacent to a possible Mammy or Himself Chair? — YES → Avoid. Himself and Mammy may sit next to one another.* Proceed to next one.

NO ←

Are there any chairs left? — NO → Stay away from the table until told to approach.

YES ←

Ask: 'Will I sit here?'

---

* To allow swift conferring on poor behaviour going on elsewhere around the table and to present a united front if 'someone' decided they didn't like peas.

Although this may seem like overkill, it's worth at least giving it some consideration because if you did sit in the wrong seat no one would move you and it would just lead to unnecessary awkwardness.

'Will I sit here?'

'Oh … do yes. You sit there, loveen.'

Himself, apparently oblivious to what's going on, puts his foot in it.

'Where will I sit?'

'You can sit here — as you always do.'

Mammy invests the word 'always' with meaning, pointing to a chair at the extreme end of the table. Himself sits on it gingerly, examining the progress of his backside as if he's afraid there may be a trap somewhere on the chair. Politeness dictates that he will put up with it but he feels awkward in this new spot. He might as well be in a restaurant.

By this point, any self-aware guest should recognize the signs and protocol dictates that something should be said. Protocol also dictates that nothing should be done about it.

'Am I sitting in your seat, Peadar? I'll move.'

'Don't MIND him, he's grand. You stay where you are, girleen. He's FINE. Aren't you fine, Daddy?'

'Oh, I'm fine altogether.'

Himself hesitates. Nothing is in its usual place.

'What are you looking for, Daddy?'

'The salt.'

'It's right there in front of you.'

'So it is. I'm used to coming at it from another angle.'

'I can move, no problem.'

'NO, YOU'RE GRAND.'

In theory she could have moved but Mammy would have none of it. Imagine making a visitor move her plate because Himself couldn't sit in a different seat for once in his life. The mortification.

The rest of the meal is a bit more subdued as everyone wonders how they let this happen. The guest rehearses in her head the argument she'll be having when they've a moment alone.

'How could you not tell me about your father's chair?'

'I was going to but you'd already sat down.'

'I was only trying to stay out of the way. I bet she doesn't like me.'

'She prefers you to me. Will you stop?'

Meanwhile Mammy and Himself are conducting their own post-mortem.

'A grand girl.'

'Even if she did sit in my chair.'

'AH, would you stop talking about your ould chair! I hope to God she didn't run her hands under the table. You wouldn't know what she'd find.'

Not all finds in the old house are so 'organic'. After things settle down a little bit, Christmas is a perfect time to go unearthing lost treasures under beds and at the backs of wardrobes.

Poking Around

'Where did you find that? 'Magine, I didn't even know we had that.'

As they grow up and move away from home, children will experiment with a variety of different interior design philosophies in their bedrooms:

- Clean lines, 400 bolsters and pillows and a print on the wall of an owl cycling to a dance organized by other woodland animals.

- A mattress on the floor in Sydney, four gearbags, two magazines, a smell that is almost tangible and one clean sock that will be partnered with the least dirty among the other socks.

- A room which sleeps one other person, whose presence 'on the scene' Mammy is unaware of.

It doesn't matter. Now you are home in your small bed, reliving your childhood room's own particular patterns: the stripy carpet that featured in many bedrooms and covered a multitude of little accidents in its day; the wallpaper whose kitsch design would cost a fortune now if it wasn't stuck to your wall; the same damp spot on the ceiling you stared at in adolescence when you were supposed to be studying.

You lie there, savouring the stillness. And then you go rooting. Somewhere, buried among the calendars from the bank, dated 2004–2010 and the thirty-four spare duvets that Mammy is storing there just in case a busload of visitors happens to swoop, you find it. The Box.

There's always a box that contains the last of the eclectic mix of 'stuff' from childhood that was somewhere in your old room.

Everyone's box of odds and ends is different, but it's quite likely you will find some of the following:

· Tickets to that concert — the first one you went to. Remember? You went with *WhatsTheirName?* They were your best friend at the time but you grew apart and you haven't met them since Stephenses Night a few years ago and it was a bit awkward when you had nothing to say to each other.

· A school report or at least one copybook from primary school. Old school copybooks are a reminder of how certain subjects may have changed slightly in the last few years and also what a bored child might do with blank pages during the summer holidays.

January 27th

Question 25 What are the seven deadly sins?
The seven deadly sins are Lust, Gluttony, Greed, Sloth, Wrath, Envy, Pride ✓

Question 26 Why do we go to mass?
We go to mass to pray and get Communion ½

Question 27 What is a mortal sin?
A very bad sin like murder or adultery if you do not say sorry you could go to hell ½

My address is

4 Parknabealcloch Road,
Slievemuckridge East,
Ballagreolish,
Co Galway,
Connacht,
Ireland,
Europe,
Northern Hemisphere,
The World,
Earth,
The Solar System,
The Milky Way,
The Universe,
God

· Your first ID card. You are momentarily taken aback by how young you looked, how small and lean your face was compared to now. You remember how old you felt when you first brandished it to a bouncer and rattled off the year of your birth, but then he diagnosed you as having drunk too much 'POP-FLAVOURED YUMMY alcoKIDZ DRINK' and told you to go away and have some coffee.

· A letter from a teenage girl. Boys may have written letters but most teenage boys will barely have been able to articulate a preference for fried or boiled spuds, let

alone discuss inner thoughts. But the typical
teenage girl's letter about recent events in
excruciating detail, with love hearts on top of
i's nd j's, is a historical document that must
be preserved by the National Library.

Killshartryglenduff 4/8/1994

Hi James,
How are you? I am fine.
I don't care what Chloe Garvin said about shifting you at the
Beat on the Street. She is just a liar and I'm not her friend
anymore anyway since she was saying that stuff about Niamh.

Will you be at the Junction tonight? Not a big gang from school
going. Just me, Trish D, Trish C, Trish Crowley, Niamh, Yvonne,
Denise, Babs. We could go for a walk. But you don't have to or
anything.
Anyway ~~would you like to we could~~ I'll see you later I suppose.
          Trish (Trish Bergin) xxxx ~~S.W.A.L.K.~~

But you can't be doing too much poking around,
just in case you find the presents before they're
unwrapped. If they've even been bought yet.

7

Present Tension

Don't go spending your money on me now.
Something small'll do me.

Buying gifts is all about expectation management and the most expectant (and expectorant) species are children. Reams of advice have been written about how to train children to be reasonable in their Christmas wish-list. This usually involves sitting down with children well in advance, discussing what's possible, asking them to prioritize their wish-list while playing The Rolling Stones' 'You Can't Always Get What You Want' repeatedly in the background. For the last few years, Mammies have been in a position to use the Irish Government approach — namely that Mammy's hands are tied because of the ECB-IMF-European Commission Troika and the carry-on of the previous government — as a means to let children know that things are tight. Now with the mood in the country at least marginally on the up, it's harder to trot out that excuse. The remaining option is to use the Garth Brooks debacle and tell children that toys are only available subject to licence, and liable to be cancelled at the last minute.

It's important to keep alive the magic of Santa while also painting a picture of a practical Santa who is very much an ally with Mammy and Himself.

- 'Santy may not have been able to fit all the toys in his sack.'

- 'Santa delivers the presents but Mammy and Daddy have to pay for them.'

- 'Well, I was talking to MRS Claus and she said her husband put out his back last year with all the big toys so they'll have to be smaller this year. Do you remember when Daddy hurt his back?'

Nevertheless, children will have to be given something. Santa has an important role to play, especially with a strategic early visit.

In the Grotto

Just as petrol stations became 'Services', corner shops became delicatessens and shebeens became artisan food courts serving a variety of craft beers, the Santa visiting experience has changed a lot in recent decades.

Now a good Santa's grotto will be located in a forest, elves will read the queuing children a story, there will be carol-singing and mulled wine for the adults, a living crib and a farmers' market. The emphasis will be on providing a memorable experience and Santa — with real beard — will very usefully talk the children down from their 400-item list to something more manageable.

There was a time when Santa's grotto was a broom cupboard at the back of a shop next to the detergents, and a gruff-and-ready Santa handed out 'lucky' bags with a colouring book and a dinky and sent you on your way.

No wonder most families' Santa photo exuded quite a lot of tension.

Naming Rights

In other countries, if there is a debate, it's about whether he should be called Father Christmas or Saint Nicholas. The Irish language gets around this with Daidí na Nollag. For the non-gaelgóirs, it's a simple choice: is he Santa or Santy? The following guide should help.

WHAT TO CALL HIS NIBS

SANTA	SANTY
With Claus.	When asking in advance: 'What's Santy bringing?'
When speaking to someone born outside of Ireland or else they will think you are talking about an Arsenal midfielder or a prominent avant-garde Spanish Catalan chef.	When asking in retrospect: 'Did Santy bring you anything nice?'
When threatening a misbehaving child that you're going to inform on him or her to the aforementioned so he can add their name to the 'naughty list'. You could say Santy here but in order to give full weight to the threat, Santa sounds better.	For a small child who develops a very strong fear of Santa and starts to 'lose it' rapidly on entering the cave or grotto, Santy might be less threatening a prospect than Santa. Although in the case of toddler fear-tantrums, it may be better to just leave.
Any time because that's his name.	Any time you like. Because as Irish people we have retained the right to mispronounce names for people, places and things to demonstrate that after centuries of dungeon, fire, sword, guilt and troika we will never be browbeaten into anything but will take our own direction cf. Tescos, Chris Eubanks, Euros, Chicargo, 'cousints', 'crips' and 'being pecific'.

Listology

The letter to Santa has evolved over time also:

THE GOOD OLD DAYS

Dear Santa,
I would like ...
Presents? Are ya joking me?
An orange and a jay-cloth
if you were lucky.
And we were glad of it..

THE 80'S

Dear Santa,
I've been very good this year.
Can I have a Guess Who,
a bike and a surprise.

THE CELTIC TIGER

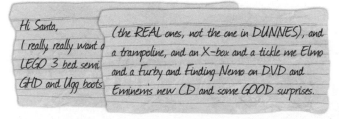

Hi Santa,
I really really want a
LEGO 3 bed semi.
GHD and Ugg boots

(the REAL ones, not the one in DUNNES), and
a trampoline, and an X-box and a tickle me Elmo
and a Furby and Finding Nemo on DVD and
Eminem's new CD and some GOOD surprises.

NOW

Tweet to Santa Claus ✕

@SantaClaus hello Santa I would like something to do
with #LOOMBANDS #FROZEN and a #SURPRISE.

📷 Add photo   47   ✒ Tweet

With the children taken care of, the focus should
turn to the most important person.

What Are We Getting Mammy?

The crucial question to ask when trying to buy Mammy's present is: What happened to the previous gifts? If the present from ten Christmases ago is still in use, has been pronounced to be A Great Yoke Altogether Without Which Mammy Would Be Bereft, then try to ascertain the secrets of its success. Conversely, what presents have remained untouched? Are books still in pristine condition? (If either of the previous *Books of Irish Mammies* look unread it's because they may be just the Good Copy; Mammy's personal copy is covered in tea spilled from laughing.)

For presents that introduced new technology into the house, is the Thing still in its box, hidden away because its presence and lack of use feels like an admonishment to Mammy? Or, even worse, is it bundled up with its cable, in exactly the same position as it was on December 27th when you tried to show Mammy how to work it, while its original box is being used to hold clippings from the local paper and old ESB bills?

What about previously gifted items of clothing? Are they in the part of the wardrobe where Mammy puts the things she'd wear again if she had the figure, or have they already been sent to Oxfam? There's your answer.

Unfortunately, this means that Mammy is often the recipient of so-called old-reliable presents — gifts given every year in the knowledge that that's what Mammy always gets. But these start to pile up and Mammy's going to have to get rid of them, one way or another.

Department of
Jobs, Enterprise and Innovation

APPLICATION FOR EXPORT LICENCE

1. Exporter: Mammy

2. Consignee: I don't care who takes them as long as someone gets the use of them. It'd be a shame to throw them out.

3. Goods
- Scarves – I've enough scarves to do me for the rest of my life.

- Bottles of sherry – you see I never drank sherry. I don't know where they got the idea I liked sherry.

- Perfume – I'd have to be Zsa Zsa Gabor to be wearing all the perfume. I'd say most of it is gone off at this stage.

- Books! If I'd nothing else to do I still wouldn't get through the books. And there's a good one there too what's its name? *The Woman, Oh The Lord Save Us! What A Difficult Life She Led, The Cratur,* I think it was called. It was on *The Late Late Show.* And that expensive one, *Fierce Big Photos Of Ireland For Putting On The Table When There's Visitors.* I mean it's lovely but it's taking up room.

4. Quantity: A rake of them.

5. End-Use: I don't mind what they do with them, as long as they're out of here.

To be absolutely sure you're getting the right thing, it's best to consult *Irish Mammy Magazine*'s exclusive gift guide.

IRISH MAMMY MAGAZINE

TAKE OUR HOLIDAY QUIZ
'Since you're so good at back-answering.'

'Ye needn't bother with any photoshoot. The state of the place.'
A SEASONAL VISIT TO MAMMY AND HIMSELF

CHRISTMAS GIFT GUIDE!
'That'll do them grand. We're not made of money.'

'I'M DISAPPOINTED IN YOU'
HOW TO HANDLE 'ACTING UP' THIS CHRISTMAS

Christmas Gift Guide

Don't be spending your money on us but if you have to get us something ...

THE WAN DIRECTION MAMMIES

MUGS

SCARFS

THE USUAL TAT

POSTERS

The true Croke Park heroes of 2014

Did your Mammy do all she could to get you to the One Direction gigs in Croke Park in 2014?

Say thanks with **The Wan Direction Mammies**, a handsomely bound, illustrated tribute to the thousands of Mammies who queued for the tickets, carried the coats, bought the *'How-much? Shur we could have made one of them!'* merchandise and the earplugs, found the parking, the right bus, and got you all home.

Mammy might have been sceptical at the start ...

But she was soon getting into the swing of things.

And not forgetting her in-built Irish Mammy training.

By the end of it Mammy was won over.

Christmas Gift Guide

May Contain Traces of Nuns!

Meditations for life and bits of religion
*(but you'd hardly notice the religion if you didn't
know it was there, so there's no panic, like).*

And for the older Mammies ...

Do you want to buy something for Mammy that suggests
you still have a bit of interest in religion or assumes that
Mammy does even if she doesn't, but still it's a nice
present all the same?

As ever, *Irish Mammy Magazine* has plenty of entertainment for all the family.

DON'T YOU LIKE QUIZZES? I COULD HAVE SWORN YOU DID. YOU MIGHT AS WELL GIVE IT A GO.

1. Were there many on the train?
2. Did you get a seat?
3. Who is the fella in the photos of the Christmas party?
4. Do you work with him?
5. Do you ever run into [local who is now in your vicinity and who Mammy holds out a forlorn hope that you might end up with]?
6. Any chance we are going to meet this girlfriend of yours?
7. What are you doing to these shirts?
8. How's the car going?
9. Have you the triangle in case you get a puncture?
10. You look different – is that the new hair?
11. Is this what you're going to be like now over the Christmas?
12. Where did you see that? Did you find that out on Facebook?
13. Did you eat the last of the biscuits? Weren't you very busy now?
14. Which one of ye is it that's gone vegetarian?
15. Ah but you'll eat a bit of turkey anyway, won't you?

The train is grand – Q1

Would I know him? – Q3

Himself has the triangle – Q9

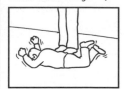
Pure Spoilt – Q11

Hippies – Q14

At home with

Mammy and Himself

It was the need to find some place to live after they first got together that ultimately led Mammy and Himself to their well-appointed, bijou, semi-detached house here on the outskirts of Kilsudgeon – a pretty, medium-sized market town which is waiting for a bypass.

Now fifteen years later they don't regret the decision to up sticks and make the big move.

'We were living with his mother but she was an awful difficult woman,' says Mammy pleasantly as we sit in the lounge.

This Christmassy room bears all the hall-marks of Mammy and Himself's creative spark. The dado rail with a rich ochre below the line and a warm tangerine yellow above the line reflects their personality.

'It's the best colour to hide the finger marks.'

We are interrupted by Mammy's rambunctious four-year-old youngest child. 'Mammy, Sophie hit me!', he wails adorably. 'Get out ye pair of scuts,' says Mammy as her husband Himself arrives in.

'Arra blast that shagging door. It's gone stuck again with the rain, the hoor,' he says cheerfully. 'They had no mix-peel left. I'm gone halfway around the country looking for stuff for this bleddy Christmas cake … Who's that?' He has noticed your reporter.

'It's the people from the magazine doing the House Bit for Christmas,' says Mammy coquettishly.

We move into the kitchen. I'm offered a mince pie. I demur, citing my diet. Himself chides, 'Arra shag the diet. Eat the bun for feck's sake and don't be looking at us making us feel bad for eating ours. C'mon there isn't a pick on you.'

The Christmas tree is in the kitchen – a novel approach. 'That's where the plugs are,' interjects Himself. 'Whoever wired this house should get a medal for being an amadán.'…. ARRA F*CK YA WILL YA LET THE BALL IN AND DON'T MIND THE FANCY DAN!' Himself breaks off as he's watching the match on a perfectly appointed Beko television which sits on top of a copy of Alex Ferguson's autobiography.

As I look at the exquisitely apportioned Christmas decorations I can see that the couple's three children have been allowed to each have an influence in the interiors of the house. 'They've made shite of the place,' says Himself proudly.

The space has a wonderful sense of flow. It is an atomic unit but also part of the community. 'We can hear every bloody thing through these walls. Such a shower of cowboys,' says Himself. 'The crowd on our left were at it hammer and tongs last night.'

And how will they spend Christmas?

'Dreading it,' says Mammy. 'His sister and the family are calling over and I don't know WHAT she's going to think of the place. The husband is rotten with money. He's after landing a big job. Vice president of Something with an American crowd.'

'And I went to school with him and he was as thick as two short planks,' adds Himself. 'But they've fierce pull.'

I reluctantly bid farewell to Mammy and Himself in their idyllic hideaway.

For good or for bad, it's done now. The presents are bought. The family members have scattered for an hour to various points of the house to wrap them. There's only one thing left.

8

All About Eve

Are you coming with me or will you go with your
father in the morning?

Christmas Eve – in some cultures the focus of Christmas celebrations and even in Ireland, the best part of 'the Christmas'. By now, everyone is home. The more stressful parts of the shopping are done. If you are a recipient of a gift bought at this stage, take it you'll be unwrapping whichever box-set or humorous book* is nearest the cash-register in the shop that's nearest the entrance to the shopping centre nearest the house because the giver 'hasn't the energy to be doing any more traipsing at this stage'.

The house has settled down now. Wrapped presents are underneath the tree. Mince pies are doing the rounds. The first box of Roses has been opened and it's not yet a chore to eat them. Visitors visit but usually they're on the way somewhere so they 'won't stay', they're 'just popping in. No honestly now,' they 'won't even sit down'. They're just leaving a bottle-shaped present that they themselves received an hour earlier.

---

* This does not apply to the *Irish Mammies* books which will have been bought with tenderness and care, far in advance of Christmas Eve. It may even have been signed with a personal dedication. Or it should have been.

Mass Attraction

Christmas Eve is also the day of Christmas Eve mass, perhaps the mass that Mammy has the least difficulty in getting children of all ages to go to. Because they know that Christmas Eve mass, as well as being a religious ceremony, is a community occasion. There is also a certain nostalgia associated with it for millennials remembering their own childhood. In some ways it's not dissimilar to *The Late Late Toy Show* — for one night at least, there's huge interest and tremendous goodwill towards an institution that used to be central to the weekends of nearly everyone. It's not held at midnight so much now, meaning most people are fairly sober, but it is still a very social event as a few months' news has to be crammed into short bursts of conversation in the cold outside afterwards. Everyone is dressed well. Mammy will not be letting them out the door shaming the family in 'those jeans'. Whether they believe the mass to be a celebration of a saviour's birth or not, everyone has a spring in their step — including the priests.

'A good few strangers in tonight,' says the priest to himself. He doesn't mind. He's not the only one to notice them.

The capacity-for-divilment part of his brain wonders if he might throw some odd instruction into the mass just to see how many of the one-per-year visitors would assume it was part of the New Mass. A thought enters his mind to ask the congregation to scratch their heads for the Lord's Blessing or stand on one foot for the Profession of Faith. But he decides against it. Priests get into enough trouble these days.

This is his favourite mass for a number of reasons:

I. The church is so full he'll get to announce rarely used contingency arrangements for communion.

EMERGENCY COMMUNION PLAN
For Christmas, Easter and Big Funerals

2. The gospel — it's a straightforward narrative and a good news story. He doesn't find himself reading any threats to the congregation about fires of hell, gnashing of teeth, there's no mention of the f-word — fornication — or telling Irish Mammies that they should be obedient at all times to Himselves. ('He'll be waiting a while for that to happen,' says Mammy into her missalette.) It's a combination of the two oldest stories in the world — the birth of a child and the difficulties in getting accommodation in a small town when there's a big event on.

3. When he says 'Happy Christmas', a few people say it back.

4. There'll be a round of applause for the choir. There is a little frisson of excitement when an Irish congregation expresses any kind of effusiveness in a church as it so rarely happens.

This choir definitely deserves the applause. They've been through a lot. There's a common thread running through voluntary activities like choirs, tag-rugby teams, Tidy Towns committees, charities: people invest a lot of themselves but when things go wrong, emotions start to run high. Quickly.

Musical Drama

'*What's. Keeping. Her?*' says Mammy to herself as she tries to get them out the door. The young lad is sitting patiently on the edge of the chair playing his DS. Mammy will have to prise that from his grasp shortly but she can't discipline one child while another is acting even more of the maggot.

Sophie has made her appearance.

'*What in the name of …*' Mammy doesn't even know which name to invoke in describing the vision at the top of the stairs. Given the rig-out, perhaps one of the Babylonian gods might be appropriate.

'What, Mammy?!' says Sophie, arming herself. She knew this would be the reaction but reasoned that by delaying the revelation of her outfit enough, Mammy would be forced to bring her anyway.

> 'You're NOT singing in the choir on Christmas Eve looking like Miley Whatsername. PUT ON SOME CLOTHES. Where's the thing I got you in Debenhams? That'll do you grand.'

The 'thing' Mammy got her would not do at all, at least not in the fantasy playing out in Sophie's mind about how tonight's choir performance is going to go.

Muttering, Sophie traipses back to her room to change. Mammy could hardly blame her for a little fuss. The choir was a hotbed of intrigue. They were on their third choir leader in a year. The previous two had exited the altar in dramatic fashion.

First there was John Tunley, a self-confessed fan of the Tridentine Mass. Mammy could tell he even made Father Rourke nervous in case he caught him out on some obscure clause of doctrine.

He was no fan of modern church music and wanted them all singing in Latin. 'Guitars on the altar are an ABOMINATION to church music,' he said. And that was the end of the choir for Niamh Storey, who had just started to take her own instrument out of its case. 'It's like having Simon Cowell looking at you. Simon Cowell in an anorak,' she said before storming out.

But after all of that didn't he run off with Pat Deegan's wife and the two of them now living over in the New Estates? 'He must have been putting secret messages in the Latin,' said Pat afterwards.

Then there was Rita Shanahan who could best be described as 'emotional'. She introduced herself by saying 'I'm a perfectionist'.

They'd be singing away when she would stop them. 'It's not WORKING, people!' she would bellow in exasperation. [Clap-clap] 'From the TOP again.' One evening Deirdre Halligan piped up from the back, in a stage whisper that, thanks to the excellent acoustics, was audible throughout the church: 'Does she think she's with the Bolshoi?'

It became tenser after that.

> 'I DON'T UNDERSTAND WHAT THE
> PROBLEM IS, PEOPLE.'

> 'It's just that some of the notes are a little
> high for us, Rita.'

> 'When I want your input I'll ask for it.'

Rita lasted another two weeks and then sent everyone a passive aggressive email citing 'musical differences' as the reason for her departure. Mammy heard afterwards that Rita was suffering from nerves so she felt bad and sent her a mass card.

The new fella is LOVELY. The guitars are back. He's all smiles and encouragement. When the harmonies worked one day, he was beaming:

> 'Lovely hurling, ladies.'

> 'Camogie, Brian.'

> 'Camogie is right, Pauline.'

But Sophie was less impressed in the car on the way home from the last practice.

> 'Mammy, you're gross. You totally fancy
> him. I'm telling Daddy.'

'He wouldn't mind a bit. He's always saying I should explore my options.'

'Stoppit, Mammy, you are disGUSTING. Not EVEN JOKING. Anyway, you're wasting your time. He's gay.'

'He is NOT.'

'He so IS, Mammy! Sorry to disappoint you. Katelynn saw him in town with his boyfriend.'

'Could be his brother.'

'Not the ways Katelynn saw it. OMIGOD Mammy, look at you! You're disappointed.'

That girl did not show enough respect. When she thought of what would happen if she spoke to her own Mammy like that …

Anyway, now she is back at the top of the stairs.

'There you are now. Like Katherine Jenkins.'

'This dress is, like, a miscarriage of justice, Mammy.'

Where do they learn this stuff? It must be from *Glee*. We didn't hear anything like that on *MacGyver*.

But she wore it and in fairness the girl could sing, although there were a few glances exchanged during 'Silent Night' when she went all Beyoncé and finished about four seconds after everyone else. Other than that, the choir gets their round of applause and everyone agrees the new choir fella is a great improvement — although *his* Mammy has a thing or two to say...

Meet and Greet

Afterwards Father is saying hello to all the people. It's bittersweet, as they'll all be asking him where he's spending Christmas and what with a few arrangements falling through he'll be alone, but there's a couple of good films on and he's going to do a bit of a binge on *Orange Is The New Black* which he's heard is 'fierce altogether'.

'Hello, Father, that was a lovely mass.'

'Ah, Mrs Grogan; how are you?'

'You know Brian, of course.'

'Indeed I do. What a beautiful job you've done with that choir. I thought we were going to have to hold a Special Dáil Inquiry to investigate it at one stage.'

'Ah, they were all great when I found them, just a bit of tweaking.'

'And THIS is Trevor, Father. Brian's *partner*.'

'Trevor, Happy Christmas to you.'

'Hello, Father, and same to yourself.'

'And they're getting *married in August*, Father. Isn't that great?'

'That's … mighty news, congratulations … lads.'

'An awful shame they have to have the whole ceremony in the Garraclough Hotel, Father. Wouldn't it be lovely to have the service here? But shur, of course, *it isn't allowed.*'

'Er … well … I suppose …'

'Ah, Mammy, leave the man alone on Christmas Eve. He's not going to change the law now. Sorry, Father, Happy Christmas, Father. *[He steers Mammy out the door.]* Honestly Mammy, when did you get so activist?'

'I just don't like anyone standing in the way of my son.'

'I can see where you get it from, Brian.'

'Don't you start, Trevor.'

Meanwhile, having survived the dispute on canon law, Father is standing there thinking of a few cans.

Believe It or Not

Mammy is buzzing after the singing. She had her own motives for being in the choir. She thought it might be a nice way to spend time with Sophie. She wondered if she really knew her daughter at all after accidentally glimpsing a photo on SnapChat ...

She had been half-hoping the music would kick off whatever bit of faith she had left herself. Her own mother was always on at her about the lack of religion. Madame upstairs seemed to make a speciality of dropping clangers which nearly sent Nana off to Lourdes for the sole purpose of praying for her descendants' souls. Like that conversation earlier in the year:

> 'No, I will not have a Creme Egg. Would you not go off them for Lent?'

> 'What's Lent, Nana?'

Mammy still cringes at the memory. It wasn't the first *faux Passover*. When they moved into the house years ago just before Christmas, she forgot one vital detail:

> 'And this is the sitting-room — we only have a few decorations up as we're just finding our feet.'

'Ye don't have the crib up yet.'

'… No, Mammy, eh … not yet. Tomás is getting one on Tuesday.'

'Am I?'

'Remember I said you had to go to town to get a few bits and pieces?'

She looked at Tomás with her 'not now' face. Tomás smiled back. He was enjoying this, the fecker. It was alright for him coming from a family of outright pagans. He didn't understand the delicate waltz between her and her mother about how much religion was still being kept up.

Nana never had to buy a crib. Her one had been a wedding present fifty years ago. It was so old, Nana used to say that the figure of Melchior was 'the first black man in this family until Auntie Rita married Lloyd in Croydon'. Nana said you wouldn't dare give a crib now: 'MTV Cribs more like, the way the houses are.' (Nana watched MTV Cribs one night because she thought it was one of those home improvement shows.)

And then Tomás had gone to Veritas for the crib and gone a little mad on 'paraphernalia' as he called it. But now after belting out the favourite tunes for an hour and getting a round of applause, Mammy's practically ready for devotions. Well, maybe one step at a time.

News of the World

Lest there be any doubt, Santa's existence is confirmed by no less august a presence than The News Reader. As mentioned in previous books, in a world where virtually no celebrity can resist the temptation to pop up elsewhere acting the eejit, Ireland's news readers have been relatively restrained.

Google them. Relative to other jobs on the telly, when it comes to a jobbing newscaster, you are less likely to read about their quest to find love, hear them profess how happy they are with their new hunk ('She's my rock/puts manners on me/etc.') or see them celebrity-judging anything. While the local correspondents may end up being press-ganged into judging Miss Macra's or welly-throwing competitions, the newscasters stay relatively aloof. They'll give a little smile at the end as they chat to the sports star. They are tantalizingly aloof. And we prefer it that way.

But there's one time when they put on the teacher-on-sports-day act: Christmas Eve. After a shortened news featuring one last story of the year about Anglo Irish Bank, they give a little smirk and announce that they have exclusive footage of Santa leaving the North Pole. As children grow older and realize the real Santa would have left hours before, the effect fades somewhat but there's something utterly believable about a newsreader telling you about Santa. Santa's sleigh looks a bit small to hold all the toys in the world but you skip over that. In fact if you look closely, you imagine you can spot a 'Surprise'-shaped object peeping out of one of the bags at the back.

> 'WhatareyoustilldoingupIthoughtItoldyou togotobedSantydoesn'tbringtoystochildren whoarenotintheirbeds! UP THEM STAIRS. NOW!'

9

The Day That's In It

Right! We're all going to have a. NICE. TIME.
IS THAT CLEAR?

Every year Mammies tell themselves it's just another day. But the presence and presents of so many people can cause drama. However, the occasion is also punctuated by moments of family togetherness, the memories of which help keep spirits up during the dull days of January and February. In short, Christmas Day is still a day like no other.

An Early Start

The alarm goes. Well, not exactly an alarm clock, just a child stirring in their sleep, knocking Teddy off the bed. Teddy's soft landing on the carpet wakes up the child, who, realizing what day it is, erupts out of the duvet like a camouflaged soldier from a pile of leaves. This sets in train an unstoppable momentum that the adults in the house will spend the next few hours trying to control.

But someone is a little subdued.

'What's the matter, pet?'

'I didn't get anything from Santa.'

'But you're eleven. You said yourself that you were a bit old for Santa.'

'Yeah, but maybe he might have given me a surprise. I don't think there IS A SANTA.'

'There is SO a Santa, and keep your voice down.'

Mammy realizes that this child is going through the difficult Santa transition phase, which can be far more traumatic than puberty. This situation needs to be managed carefully in case it destabilizes the delicate Santa balance in the house because there's a smaller child who DOES SO believe in Santa and has just made a discovery.

'MAMMY, SANTY FORGOT THE BATTERIES!'

'Yeah, Mammy, how come Santy forgot the batteries?'

'Watch it, you. Santy told me to get the batteries because he's not carrying them this year for fuel efficiency reasons, because he's trying to be environmentally friendly.'

'But they're reindeers, Mammy. They don't have petrol.'

'Well, Rudolph has to cut down on his carbon hoofprint.'

Luckily the eleven-year-old intervenes by bringing up a subject that is never far from the minds of eleven-year-olds.

'Yeah, and if they had to carry less stuff it wouldn't be as heavy so they'd fart less and farts are greenhouse gases.'

'HAHA SMELLY REINDEER FARTS PLBLBLB! PLBLBLBL!'

While the two children happily explore the possibilities and implications of reindeer farts, Mammy scoots upstairs and does a bit of rooting around and what does she find? Only a small present that must have fallen out of Santa's pocket when he sat on the settee to have his biscuits and isotonic energy drink?*

> 'You see, Santa knows you're a bit older so he got you a more grown-up present.'

She just needs to have a word with Himself about what happened to his €25 One4All voucher.

Impossible to Buy for

It's not all one-way traffic for children. The first time they buy a present independently – or with a bit of strategic assistance – for a parent is a proud moment.

It's a well-known fact that shopping for Himselves can cause a lot of stress but it's worth it because it often provides the most touching moments at present-opening times.

---

* Years of advertising have persuaded these children that Santa is wasting his time with milk and he needs 'instant hydration' for 'peak performance'.

'Whose presents are we going to open first?'

'I'll go first—'

Says Himself, picking one from the pile. The child is bouncing around with excitement.

'THAT'S MY ONE. OPEN IT OPEN IT OPEN IT!'

'What's this now? A small box. Hardly an engagement ring, I suppose. Haha.'

'NO, Daddy, c'mon, open iiit!'

'OH, it's a penknife. That'll come in handy.'

'Look, Daddy, it's got a scissors in it.'

'Perfect for cutting off your nose and ears. C'MERE!'

'No, Daddy, hahaha.'

[Wrestles and squeals ensue.]

Daddy already has a penknife but one day he uses this one and spends years telling everybody what a handy present it was, even though the scissors broke on first use.

The other successful present for Himself is the Practical Present From Mammy That He Needed And Will Definitely Get The Use Out Of.

Mammy: 'And this is from me—'

Himself [*reading out loud*]: '"From MAMMY with love."'

Children: 'Kiss kiss kiss.'

Mammy: 'Ah will ye stop, it isn't *Blind Date*.'

[*Short Mammy–Himself kiss follows.*]

Himself: 'Right, what's this now? A trousers and … oh, it's a new pyjamas.'

Mammy: 'I thought I'd get you a new pair — the ones you had were a disgrace.'

This present was already discussed repeatedly at bedtime so there's no huge surprise. On the other hand, a new pyjamas is a symbol of comfortable togetherness and a reminder for small children that not all presents are for them. And it has a grand pocket in the shirt for his glasses.

As a present buyer, Himself's record is patchy. Often it's delegated to Mammy to do the present buying as she has access to places that Himself might feel a little uncomfortable wandering around. Coupled with the fact that the present was on a list, this leads to a very knowing exchange between Daddy and his teenage daughter when she selects her next present for opening.

'OK, my turn! What's this?' ... Oh, I think
I know. It's ... a King of Skin, Body Butter,
Exfoliation and Conditioner set. Thank
you, Daddy.'

'I knew you'd like it.'

'Very thoughtful, Daddy.'

'I know, I was all day picking it out, wasn't I,
Mammy?'

'You were. We couldn't get you out of the
place, you were nearly going to buy a load of
bath bombs.'

A far more interesting present is the one to the
teenage daughter from First Serious Boyfriend.

'And this is from Stephen to me.'

Himself and Mammy will be particularly keen to get
a look at this. They will try to glean some evidence
of the progression of the relationship and of his
character. If it looks expensive he's not sensible,
a bit flighty. If there's too little expense, he's a
cheapskate. If the boyfriend is local, assumptions
can be made about what kind of stock he came from.

'No surprise there wasn't much spent on
that. You wouldn't see Paddy parting with
much. Rotten with money and still driving
the Carina.'

Of course, true evidence of his character could have been gleaned from the secret presents they gave each other earlier in the holidays – the ones that are not safe to be viewed by the family, especially as that could have resulted in explanations like: 'No, Nana, it's not a hair straightener.'

Now it's Mammy's turn.

> 'A scarf! Ah thanks pet. That'll go with my … anyway … I'll find something to wear with it.'

> 'Wait, Mammy, there's a box with it.'

> 'What's this?… A phone. But I have a phone.'

> 'It's a smartphone Mammy. From all of us.'

> 'A. Smart. Phone. It'll be my turn to get smart with ye now haha. Well thanks ever so much. Ye're very good … Now! Let ye clear all this away. I've to get the dinner started.'

By 'this' Mammy means the detritus of the morning – wrapping paper, bedsocks that have slipped off, toys on the floor that would give a Health and Safety officer a conniption. She could equally be referring to people. For a Mammy who is doing the Christmas dinner, she needs the evacuation, from under her feet, of all non-essential personnel.

Some slump off to the television, others to fight over the toys and many go to take part in the rituals – old and new – that happen on Christmas Day.

Ritual Reality

Some go to Christmas morning mass. Although the story is the same, the tone of Christmas mass is different to the one the night before. Something has happened overnight, depending on your belief system — The Birth, The Good News or, for some, just Santa. There is a further update on last night's wardrobe if this morning's presents are wearable. Neighbours can see and greet each other now with warmth. Some of the anticipation and tension that was there on the eve has evaporated. It's also a mass with no Sunday newspapers after it, so there's no bad headlines about malfeasance in the semi-state sector to spoil the morning.

As time has gone on other rituals have taken up the time of those who don't go en mass. On the beaches, charity swims bring hundreds of giggling, wobbly, blotchy humans tiptoeing across the stones, interspersed with the lean presence of a few people who are 'big into triathlons' and the gloriously freckled, barnacled, grey-haired wonder that is an ould lad's back. Thousands of people take part in charity miles along the roads and parks of the country. They arrive home full of endorphins and with blood racing, vowing to kick winter in the proverbials and go for a bracing walk every day from now on — a habit that ends on New Year's Day.

Also out and about is the Stalwart Mammy. In community halls up and down the country, there are Mammies manning the pots, ladling out the Christmas dinner to those for whom the day might be a bit lonely.

> *[Whispers]* 'Here he comes now. The cratur. I remember when he came around here first he was the bee's knees. He'd be going around doing jobs.'

> *[Whispers]* 'And you know there's a bit of work now but he's gone off the deep end altogether with the drink. Whisht, here he comes now and he still has the hat godblesshim.'

> 'Now, Dimas — you're all style.'

> 'I make special effort to see you, Anita.'

> 'You're a divil! So charming all the time, Dimas.'

> 'It's all I have left. I have nothing else.'

Mammy flinches a little when she hears him say that and she tries to steer him away from that kind of talk as she doles out the mash.

> 'Ah, don't be like that now, loveen, there's plenty left for you.'

> 'Maybe.'

'Where is it you're staying these days?'

'I stay with Sandor — Hungarian guy. We go fishing maybe later. So when are you going to divorce your husband and go with me? I bring you back to Belarus.'

'Haha! You fecker. I can't divorce him yet — I want to be sure of getting the house. It's all tied up with the solicitor.'

'I build you a new house.'

'I'd be waiting for that, I'd say. Now will you have carrots and stop your oul talk.'

'He is lucky man.'

'I'll tell him you said that. Now, a bittaturkeynham?'

'A bit of you, Anita.'

'Stop that now, Dimas, or you'll get no pudding.'

They watch as Dimas walks over to a table with his chums.

'You've an admirer there.'

'Ah, he's harmless. Although I suppose you've to be careful in case they'd get the wrong idea.'

'He's a few pals anyway. Is that Sandor there?'

'The best plasterer you could ever meet, according to Himself. Says Jimmy Partlin got him in to do something. A pure artist for plastering, Jimmy says. He was nearly personally insulted by the job the previous fella had made of the wall, not knowing of course that it was Jimmy who'd plastered it. And Jimmy didn't let on. And the whole lot of them now are living over in that NAMA place. Nothing to do all day only go fishing and drink cans. And a few Irish lads gone in too for good measure. No women in their lives, that's the problem, you see. Here's Paddy the Weatherman now.'

'Now, Paddy. Happy Christmas to you. Bittamash?'

'Cold enough out.'

''Tis, Paddy. Cold enough. Still, I suppose better than last year with the storms. How are you?'

'Yesterday was milder.'

''Twas, Paddy. It got cold overnight.'

'The forecast is for rain but it might hold off.'

'It might, Paddy. You'll eat a bit of cabbage.'

'No El Niño this year.'

'I wouldn't know much about El Niño now, Paddy. Are we better off without it?'

'A hoor of a thing, El Niño.'

'I hope we don't get a dose of it over here. We've enough to be going on with. You'll have the jelly and custard for after. You will. There you go now, Paddy. Have a lovely Christmas.'

'Last Christmas was mild too.'

Paddy continues muttering meteorologically as he shuffles back to the table. The Mammies stand watching him, ladles in hand.

'El Niño. Where does he come up with it?'

'He's mad into El Niño since he started reading the *National Geographics*. Himself was stuck talking to him an hour one day during the summer, telling him about fracking in Montana.'

'Fracking and El Niño. He's like our foreign correspondent.'

'Only he never leaves the town.'

Meanwhile other dinner dramas are unfolding throughout the neighbourhood.

I Hope Ye're Hungry …

On the face of it, most families have a very similar Christmas food-wise but if you look closer, there are tiny variations between houses. It's like the difference between language and dialect.

A starter no less

No one eats a starter in their own home unless there are visitors, but Christmas is different. Somewhere along the way — maybe when the home was being set up first — it was decided there should be a starter, and this remains unchanged for decades. In its own way it preserves the food fashion of the time of its inception. Thus, the prawn cocktail is safe for another few years yet. Unless a new tradition is adopted.

The strange food

Like any dialect, foreign influences can take hold and be surprisingly resilient no matter how incongruous they may be.

At some point during the difficult years a teenager might decide that Mammy and Himself are UNBELIEVABLY STUPID AND BORING and the clearest manifestation of this is the conservatism around the Christmas dinner. This situation should be handled carefully, much earlier, at the planning stage:

'I'll make the starter, Mammy.'

'Are you sure now?'

'WHY DON'T YOU HAVE ANY FAITH IN ME?'

'Well … it's just that …'

'IT'S JUST THAT WHAT?'

'Well … I just hope we're not going to have a repeat of the Blue Potatoes.'

Mammy is referring here to an incident two Christmases ago when a certain teenage child dyed a certain top dark blue using a certain pot, didn't wash the pot properly and then the pot was used for boiling potatoes which subsequently turned out the same colour as the upcycled top.

'Ah, Mammy.' *[Eye roll]*

'What were you thinking of making?'

'I'm doing sushi rolls.'

'We'll hardly have room for it after the prawn cocktail.'

'We can have sushi instead. You have to broaden your horizons, Mammy.'

'I see. My horizons. Would I get these rolls in SuperValu?'

'Mammy! If you don't make it from scratch it defeats the whole purpose.'

Mammy wonders which purpose needs to be defeated.

'I suppose it does.'

'I'LL get the ingredients. OMIGOD this is going to blow your mind.'

Christmas Day, noon:

'ARE YOU GETTING UP OR WHAT TO MAKE THESE SUSHIS? YOUR FATHER IS ANXIOUS TO START THE DINNER.'

'Unnhunh?'

'These SUSHI rolls you were to make.'

'Unnhunh?'

'Do you want me to make them?'

'Unnhunh.'

Two hours later:

'These sushis are not bad at all. Thanks for your suggestion. Maybe next year you'll make them yourself.'

[Eye roll]

That oven is slow today

Though not the only meat, the most popular is still turkey and the most important thing about turkey is keeping it moist. The obsession with the moistness of the turkey is such that it has even been commemorated in this poem by Prominent Irish Poet, Gabhann McGabhann:

FLESH AND BONE

Is the turkey dry she asked?
The half-light of winter solstice
glancing off her face
NO IT ISN'T, they replied as one,
all of them simultaneously
forking another slice
as if to prove its moistness
was like a drug
as if the slices
were off-white gold
But she was not to be persuaded and
lamented the drought that
she was convinced had
ravaged the bird
as if it lay dead in a parched wadi
in Northern Kenya
where she had a brother
a priest.

King of the Belgians

Rather like the Saturnalia festival itself, Christmas is a time when those normally unwelcome at the table are given pride of place. Once Christmas is over, they are scorned. And so it is with Brussels sprouts. They appear in the house after the First Big Shop, crouching demurely in their little red net bag, going through the eight stages of the Brussels sprouts life-cycle.

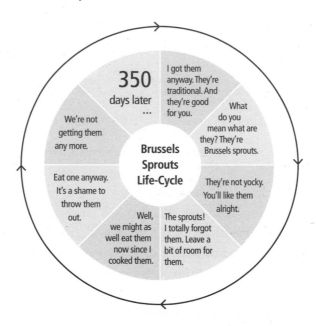

In the greater scheme of things, though, a few forgotten Brussels sprouts are quite immaterial. As Mammy is often heard to say — there's worse off in the world.

Time tables

Every family has their own Christmas Dinner Time. This can lead to a phenomenon later in the day known as the Accumulated Christmas Dinnertime Conversation or AC/DC. This is where Mammies ask each other about dinner time.

'Oh, hello, how are you? I thought it might be you. Well, Happy Christmas. How's it going? Oh, we're fine here. Just had our dinner. And ye? Oh, not till then? There'll be no rush, so ... What's that? That's a good idea. A bit of a walk to work up the appetite. That's good. A GOOSE? Aren't ye very *Downton Abbey* haha? First catch your goose as they say haha. I don't know when I had a goose last.'

'Oh, hello, how are you? I thought I'd give a quick ring before the dinner. Oh ye've had the dinner already?! Aren't ye very wise? Great to get it out of the way … Yes … yes and relax then for the afternoon. The Cregans haven't even had the dinner yet. Six o'clock they're doing it! Isn't that very late? I'd be tossing in my bed all night. A goose if you don't mind. Ye're having beef? Very nice. I like the beef myself now.'

'Oh, hello, how are you? Oh, are ye in the middle of the dinner? A good time to have it. Because I was talking to Mrs Cregan and they weren't having it until SIX, 'magine! And then the Foleys had theirs eaten and cleared away by half one. That's a bit early now for me. They had beef. And the Cregans had goose. I know, GOOSE! I said to her that they were like *Downton Abbey*. … What's that? Oh, we had the turkey. Same as ever.'

Anything good on?

Dinner over, time to see what's on the box. The old reliable is wheeled out. *The RTÉ Guide* on Christmas Day still has relevance. Most of the television it previews has yet to happen. But it is getting dog-eared. It has already lost its cover. Here it is if you have forgotten what it looks like.

Your Christmas Day Viewing!

The Usuals

A Gameshow!
Oh the craic! Six celebs make sense of the year that's gone by in a show we've put together at the last minute but shur we'll see how they get on anyway. This stuff isn't easy and I don't see you sticking your neck out.

Urbi et Orbi
Whisht! It's the Pope. You wouldn't know what he'd say next.

The News
It's the short news. A bit from Urbi et Orbi, Michael D. Higgins, the Forty Foot and some awful thing that's after happening abroad, the craturs.

The Films

Loads of Acting
A stirring portrayal of a serious topic and fierce acting, fellas with beards and women with big coats. She carries him through the snow and ... then the dog ... Oh the poor dog.You'd feel sorry for the dog.

Big Expensive Fillums
It's a Disney one – the one they were all on about. So put away that iPad for once and just watch it now because we paid a rake of money for it.

The Quare Film on Late
There'll be no one up for this one apart from the young lad. Claudette Fontainebleu-Chevalier stars as a frustrated architect trapped in a loveless marriage when a mysterious intern with floppy hair and strong arms arrives to do a bit of data entry and timesheets. If no one watches it, we don't mind. We bought the DVD in Enable Ireland for a euro.

The Soaps

Fair City

McCoys is closed so the houses of Carrigstown are very crowded, leading to tense family-related situations. Dean has a secret. Wayne knows what it is. Barry has gotten shook looking. Niamh is up to her old tricks. Ah Paul! What are ya doing? Ciara has a face on her. His Nibs is back! He was gone out of it for a while after he got a bit of work on *Vikings*. A guard arrives at the door. Howya Guard.

Coronation Street

Tyrone! He's comical, isn't he? But it's a sad Christmas for him as Fiz tells him she's moving to *Midsomer Murders*. Roy Cropper is puzzled. Some of the newer characters have another row. Poor Alf Roberts. He went very sudden, didn't he, that time?

Red Rock

That's that new one, is it? Sure we'll have a look at it anyway, I suppose.

Emmerdale

The Dingles! You couldn't be up to them. I can hardly keep track of them all. And in case any Himselves ask, Alan Turner died last year and, yes, it did go downhill after the plane crash.

EastEnders

It's dramatic times as usual down Walford way as they are all in the Queen Vic celebrating but little do they know there's a huge disaster about to happen. An asteroid or something. Meanwhile Greg shouts when he finds out about the affair.

'How could you do that?'
'I'm sorry, babes, it just … happened.'
'BUT WITH MY BEST FRIEND, AND MY MUVVER!'
'I know, babes. If I could turn back time I really would.'

Meanwhile the sound of singing from the Vic filters through the walls. Someone has a chat outside even though it's freezing. There's an explosion and everyone rushes outside. DUN DUN DUN DO DO DO DOOO DEE DOOO …

Watching all of this telly is hungry work.

It is early evening. The sky barely got bright before the sun sloped off again, half a day's work done. Everyone is in from the walks, course fifteen of the dinner — The Roses — has been served. The Film is on, watched by one person trying to hear the dialogue and half-watched by all the others who are playing with/reading presents or checking if someone has liked their Instagram of their dinner. This is peak-Christmas.

It is often at this time that some older Mammies, protected from the cold and gurriers by a phalanx of two or possibly three generations of descendants gathered around them, feel at their most alone.

Soon Nana is called in to enjoy another instalment of her favourite soap. It looks like Steve McDonald is in for the fifty-eighth disappointment of his *Coronation Street* career. And, maybe, Nana might join Mammy for a little drink. Just a little one. She doesn't want to be 'on her ear'. But it's just one day.

10

That's it Now, for Another Year

It flew, didn't it?
Oh it did. It flew.

It really was just one day. After the 25th is over, the house exhales a little. Tension is released. Gradually the family starts to broaden its horizons. And get some fresh air.

A Bit of Fresh Air

Mammy has to get out of it. There's too many in the house, much and all as she likes having them home. And the clutter! Not a one of them seems to remember how to bring their own stuff up to their rooms … What's more, Himself's mother was over for the Christmas and there was a frank and open exchange of views.

Mammy needs a walk and a debrief. Pat Roche is the woman to go for the walk with. Normally Mammy would have just rung her:

> 'H— Hello, it's me. How are ye?
> HaveagoodChristmas? … That's good … Oh nottoobadthankgod … Listen Pat, will we go for a walk? … I'll tell you all about it … Oh haha, very hush-hush.'

This year, though, she has tried to text her on the new phone.

Mammy
Just now

Oh **Pat Roche** will u take me out of here haha.
Going spare between himself's mother and the
young lads my head is melted. Will we go for a
walk out the Old Road?

'Mam! Did you mean to write that on
Facebook?'

'Write what on Facebook?'

'What you said to Pat Roche.'

'FACEBOOK? That was a text.'

'I think you clicked on the wrong app.
You've just put it on her wall on Facebook.'

'But I thought it was … I pressed the … This
BLOODY PHONE.'

'You'd better delete it.'

'I will.'

But Mammy continues to struggle with the new gadget.

Mammy
Just now

melted. Will we go for a walk out the Old Road?

Himself

'Oh Mammy, you've just posted again with a photo of yourself and tagged Daddy in the post. Will you turn off the camera on the phone?'

'Tagged? What do you mean?'

'Give me your phone, Mam. Haha you'll have the family in the papers if you're not careful.'

'This phone is too smart for me altogether.'

'Right Mammy, I've deleted it now. You were lucky I was here. By rights I should be charging you a fee for Technical Support.'

'You can take it out of my fee for raising you.'

'I should have tried to blackmail you with the photo.'

'Haha, shur there'd be no point in blackmailing me. I have nothing. I gave you everything already. I'd better go. Pat'll be waiting.'

'Look, leave me your phone. I'll change the settings in case you start accidentally tweeting about hormones or something.'

Drama over, Mammy finally meets up with Pat Roche to discuss what has been a very trying Christmas. There she is, waiting at the corner, bouncing slightly on her heels.

'You're rarin' to go, Pat.'

'I'm trying to break in these new runners. Liam bought them for me.'

'Ah, the dote. What brand are they?'

'God knows. Some oul Lidl thing. He practically forced them on me going out the door. I didn't have the heart to tell him they're already cutting the legs off me. Sure, he wouldn't know I take a wide fitting. We're martyrs to our children, Sally.'

'A sword shall pierce your heart.'

'Speaking of which, how did you get on with the Iron Lady?'

'Oh stop … It was a long Christmas.'

'She made her presence felt.'

'Presence is right … in more ways than one. You should SEE th'oul shift she got me as a gift. "This'll do you, Sally," she says. She didn't even wrap the thing. It was in one of those Tesco Bags for Life.'

'What did you say?'

'What could I say? And she smiling away at me. "You shouldn't have," I said to her. And I meant it. Does she want me to be going around like Frank McCourt's mother?'

Mammy pauses as a brightly coloured breeze of Mammies passes them in the opposite direction.

'How're the girls?'

'Not too bad.'

'Did ye have a good Christmas?'

'Quiet now. And yourselves?'

'Mayhem! Haha.'

'Are they all at home?'

'Full house.'

'That's lovely.'

'That's the way.'

'Walking off the dinner.'

'Oh stop! I'll be walking this off till the cows come home.'

'Bye bye now.'

'Tell them all I was asking for them.'

'I will.'

'Call up for a cup of tea at some stage.'

'I will.'

'It'll have to be rice cakes with the tea, haha.'

'Haha. Grand so.'

Both sets of Mammies wait for a ten-yard gap to open up before Sally opens her mouth:

'You see, I was never good enough for her. Do you know what she said to me on the wedding day?'

'You told me this before ...'

'"Look after him now. I had high hopes for Tom." High hopes, you know? And he could hardly scratch his ear without permission from her when I got him. Well, he grew up fast enough married to me, I'll tell you that much.'

'And what does Tom say about the Christmas present?'

'Ah shur, he won't say boo to her. She had them all ruined. Four grown men, you know, and they all turn into little boys around her.'

'You got through it anyway.'

'Just about. Every now and then I'd go upstairs and turn on the radio loud and sort of roar into the wardrobe. "That turkey is very dry," she'd say. "Would there be any more gravy?" or "That tea towel is dirty. Have you no clean ones?" I was THIS close to telling her what I was going to do with the tea towel.'

Meanwhile another family is about to get a visit.

Dropping In

The doorbell rings. The post-Christmas visitors are usually the best type of caller. The tension of Christmas has been broken. The visit is casual, the visitor doesn't mind squeezing themselves into the debris of wrapping paper, newspaper, new toys, books, unwanted scarves. Underneath the clutter, the house is intrinsically clean so Mammy doesn't mind. On the other hand, some Christmas visits are paid by the neighbour who brings their own special brand of Christmas cheer — the Mrs Dolans of this world.*

Mammy goes to the door. The family hear her open it and a slight pause. That's not a good sign. Mammy is usually ready for any visitors.

'Oh! MRS DOLAN, aren't you good to call?'

The family freeze. It's too late to escape. Mrs Dolan comes in — The Anti-Christmas.

'How did ye get over "the Christmas"?'

She pronounces 'Christmas' as if it were a disease picked up in an unsavoury establishment.

---

*Not her real name. None of the names in these books are anyone's real name, or if they are, they're not meant to be. In other words, Irish Mammies Industries doesn't know anyone called Mrs Dolan, although it did have a cousin a Dillon.

In awkward visitor situations like these, Mammy does two tasks at once:

- Filling the dead air with conversation:

> 'Will you have tea, Mrs Dolan? Get up there, Thomas, and let Mrs Dolan sit down. Is this your tablet? Take that out of the way as well. Sit down there, Mrs Dolan. No, no trouble at all. Sharon, take Mrs Dolan's coat there. Oh, you'll keep it to hand? Grand so. You're still recovering from that cold, I suppose.'

- Scattering glances at everybody in the room that say:

  1. Behave yerselves

  2. The Likes of Mrs Dolan were sent to try us

  3. Offer it up and it can be your good deed for Christmas

  4. She's had it hard, the poor thing, since the husband died.

Himself helps out:

> 'How was Christmas for ye?'

> 'Oh, 'twas quiet now this year.'

Mrs Dolan's Christmases are always quiet although she always sounds surprised or disappointed as if the previous Christmas was spent fighting the Taliban in Waziristan or doing meow meow with a couple of Argentinian waiters.

'Arrah, I hate all the bother of it. All the fuss.'

'I know, yeah, it's an awful lot of bother.'

Himself lies. He loves Christmas but empathizes with Mrs Dolan on foot of Instruction Number 4. Bertie Dolan was a mournful lump of a man who had needed a lot of care in his later years.

An equally lugubrious adult son Dinjo remains around the place, not doing much apart from obsessively checking the Facebook page for his small company which offers Digital Marketing Courses for Small Businesses, whose mission statement reads: *The key to catching the wave of public opinion is a successful campaign activation and Drumtyrell DigiMark is the activator your business needs.* It only has fifteen likes, though, and the most recent comment on it is from Dinjo's cousin-once-removed, calling the company 'gay'.

Mrs Dolan's roving eye lands on the nearest victim, the youngest, who is trying hard to be invisible.

'That's an awful big phone … is that a phone you have?'

'Nooo, it's an iPad.'

'An iPad! Lord God, when I think of what we used to get for Christmas. And Gary Grogan split up with the wife too.'

Mrs Dolan specializes in 'sidebar' stories that appear at intervals next to the main news report currently being aired.

'Goway! And they only three years married.'

'Ah, he had been carrying on with the young wan who does the Zumba.'

'You don't do the Zumba, Mrs Dolan?'

'Deedn' I don't do the Zumba. It's all I can do to get in and out of the chair.'

'It's supposed to be good for flexibility.'

Some of the children are trying to make the best of this situation and perhaps a campaign to get Mrs Dolan doing the Zumba might at least pass the time. Mrs Dolan puts an end to it.

'Ah, Zumba! A racket I'd say is all that Zumba is.'

Once something has been labelled a racket, that's it. Mammy takes up the baton.

'Were there many home for the Christmas, Mrs Dolan?'

'Ah, just Dinjo. Very quiet. A whole load of fuss for one day.'

'You were up at the graveyard. How is it up there?'

'They've the whole place ruined up there, digging it up.'

'I heard they were relandscaping it. It'll be nice when it's done.'

'Ah, relandscaping! Why did they have to go near it?'

Mrs Dolan is not a believer in the maxim that you can't make an omelette without breaking an egg. For her it's a case of 'Omelettes, is it? Aren't you very fond of yourself?'

'And I suppose it's oul video games, is it?'

It's back to the iPad.

'*Minecraft*. I'll show you.'

And then the youngest, like an animal that hasn't acquired enough knowledge of humans yet to be afraid, approaches Mrs Dolan with the iPad.

Something strange happens. For nearly ten Christmases Mrs Dolan has been coming in, dousing the house with her own particular brand of festive spirit, but maybe what has been missing all along was to be shown a game on an iPad that allows her to burrow into caves to gain shelter from monsters.

'You just punch those rocks. Just punch. Yeah, like that.'

'Did I do it right?'

'Yeah, and now you have coal. You pick up the coal and then you have to put it in your storage box.'

'Coal for the fire.'

'Yeah, but you need logs to make torches. To fight the zombies.'

'Zombies. And where do they come from?'

'I dunno. They just come out at night. That's why you've to do everything during the day, 'cos you won't be able to hardly see them and then they sneak up and you've to kill-um or they'll suck all the life out of you.'

'I've one of those at home.'

Was that a smile? The rest of the family is transfixed. They're afraid to say anything, to break the spell of this moment. The youngest gets agitated.

'Quick – there's the zombies! Use the hammer.'

'What hammer?'

'The one you got for your toolbox. Remember, you punched the crate?'

'Where's the toolbox? Aaagh! He's all over me. He was too quick for me with my arthritis.'

'They've killed you. But you can start again. Wait, I'll get it started.'

Himself can't resist.

'Will you be getting an iPad yourself now, Mrs Dolan?'

She pauses for a second.

'I don't know, bit-of-a-cod ... I see the bank have taken the shop off the Carrigans.'

Baby steps.

On the Feast of Stephenses

The office party is with your work colleagues; the twelve pubs is with the work colleagues you may actually like; Christmas Day is for your family; but in some ways, Stephenses night is for the neighbours.

It's as if some modern-day Herod has ordered all people to return to the pub of their birth to register the latest changes in their lives. And it's entirely possible the innocents could get slaughtered at the end.

It's an important début for the young adult coming home from the first job abroad. The Town needs to know whether the choices made have been the correct ones. In fact, The Town may harbour a secret hope that the choices made were the wrong ones. Mammy could also throw a spanner in the works.

> 'I'm going out myself tonight. You never know, I might bump into ye around town … Oh, the look of HORROR on your face!'

> 'Don't even think about it, Mam. Like … I can't even right now … I just can't EVEN …'

> 'You might see your poor mother enjoying herself for once — going mad in … what is that place ye go to — Club Ikon, is it?'

> 'You'd hate that place Mammy — the music is too loud.'

> 'Oh, I don't know — I could be twerking away to bate the band.'

> 'I KNOW WHAT YOU'RE DOING, MAMMY.'

'Oh, thelordsaveus, girleen, you're fierce easily risen. And you're the one doing Media Studies.'

The smaller the town, the more likely that Mammy will bump into one of her brood. The age spread in the local pub makes it like the Queen Vic or the Rovers Return. It is also a tapestry of so many encounters, full of half-talk and sideways glances at Who's Home From Abroad. People who haven't seen each other since secondary or even primary school are thrust together in the small confines of the local pub. Judgements are made in the blink of an eye. Those who left and came back with their haircuts and good skin from a life in a healthy climate look in satisfaction at lads who are greying and paunching, while from the other side it's clear Yer Man Thinks He's The Dog's Proverbials. There are awkward encounters with first boyfriends and girlfriends. You could arrive home as newly promoted Vice President of Mergers and Acquisitions, EMEA Region and have the rug pulled from under you when you bump into someone who you practically BEGGED for a shift.

Stephenses night is so laden with meaning that it's a wonder Irish poets aren't queuing up to write about it. So much happens between the lines, it would be a shoo-in for the Leaving Cert syllabus next to 'Digging' and Austin Clarke's 'The Planter's Daughter'.

Stephenses

The girl stares at her, placing her, like her mother would do.
She approaches. She 'has her now'. I knew your brother.
He was in the same class.
Amanda, isn't it? That's right and – ah, you're Denise.
I remember you coming over asking Mammy
For a Mister Freeze. You were small I suppose you don't
Remember. You're in Dublin now.
That's right, and yourself?
Oh here now for my sins. We've a house
Built up the road, next to Brendan's Mother.
I've two small ones now.
Oh you've your hands
Full. She agrees about her hands being
Full. Oh, stop the lights. Don't be talking to me.
After the lights stop, there is a pause. Inevitably.
Any kids yourself?
No not yet.
Sympathy. Ah Shur there's plenty of time.

Irina is being introduced to the lads.
Tell me Irene, howdidyouendupwiththisbollox? Her name
Mispronounced already.
We meet in Zurich she says
I thought it was San Fran ye were in. Following the Big
Money, Hah? He laughs. He is following the big money.
Not that he'd let on to these feckers.
With their Skodas.

New Year's Eve

'Can't you stay in and have your few drinks here? And if you wanted to have people over ... nottoomanymind.'

Megan takes the plunge. She'll take Mammy up on the offer. There's never been a party here before. She makes a mental note to hide some of the slabs in her room in case Mammy would make some remark about them having been to the Cash 'n' Carry. She also has to decide who to have over. Can she trust Kyle – the mentalist? He did a shot through his eye at the Traffic Lights Ball. WHAT's he going to say to Mammy? Maybe he'll make Megan look sensible by comparison. Anyway, it won't be for long.

'But we'll probably head into town after.'

'Oh, do whatever ye want. We'll stay out of yere way.'

But it doesn't work out like that. It is impossible for a youngster's party to take place in a house with an Irish Mammy present without some cross-pollination occurring.

At the start, Mammy is in 'Fine and happy for herself' mode but it doesn't stay that way for long.

'Sorry, I was just looking for the bathroom, Mrs Cooney.'

'Up the stairs, first on the left. I don't think I've met you before ...'

'I'm Kyle.'

'Oh, so YOU'RE the famous Kyle. Are you the lad that's doing the computer games?'

'Yah ... I do a bit, yah.'

'Aren't ye great making a go of it now? With the brother, isn't it? What is it ye call yerselves – eh, Cathy-something?'

'Catharsys, yah. Lovely place ye have here.'

'Ah, we do our best. As long as you don't look too closely ha, isn't that the way?'

...

'And I heard on the news there that the whole gaming thing is going to take off they say. Not a bad business to be in. I suppose you're a real whizz at all those yokes now.'

Kyle's heart flutters and his hand involuntarily reaches for the small plastic bag in the back pocket of his jeans before he realizes what type of yokes Mammy means.

'Oh yeah, it's a real growth industry.'

'A growth industry — isn't that great? You'll be like your man Zuckerberg, what's it he is called. Mike Zuckerberg, is it? The fella on Facebook. Remember us now when you're a billionaire haha.'

…

'Well, nice meeting you anyway, Kyle.'

Time flies. Megan is not happy that while time has flown, her party seems to have stayed exactly where it was. She tries to inject some urgency.

'Are we heading into town or WHAT?'

No one is keen to move. Outside it's chaotic. Eighteen-year-olds are roaming the streets with Uzis and hunting dogs. Inside it's warm and cosy and …

'Now, who's for a few sausage rolls?'

MAM!!! says Megan's face. But she knows the cause is lost. Mammy has charmed all of her friends. And then the unthinkable happens. The whole party — Mammy included — find themselves watching RTÉ's coverage of the New Year's Eve celebrations. They're not the only ones. Around the country, there's a Mammy Goggle-box going on.

Back at the party:

> 'Well, did you enjoy that? Your old mother didn't show you up, did she?'

> 'No, Mammy. Thanks, Mammy.'

> 'And that boy, Kyle. He seems like a nice fella. Any kind of a story there?'

> 'MAM!'

Megan will need to have words with Kyle.

Megan Coonaiye ▸ **K-Roz**
Wtf did u say 2 my Mam. She's like Kyle dis and Kyle dat. OMG so embrasing

K-Roz Wot can I say. De older women love me

Megan Coonaiye OM Actual GOD STOPPIT

K-Roz Wot A good lukin woman ur mam

Megan Coonaiye BORK

II

Doing the Leaving

TOMORROW! I thought it wasn't for
another couple of days ...

Where Do You Think You're Going?

'Is it over already?' asks Mammy as the credits roll at the end of the film. She's not just asking about the end of the film or the day, but the beginning of the end of the Full House. As she reminds her family for the fifteenth time to unplug everything and put up the fireguard, she feels a pang. Soon there'll be no need for reminders. When it's just herself and Himself, the house runs itself but with the arrival back of the family all the old rules of the house had been dusted down and flagged. But once Christmas Day is over, it's as if the legal duty of a child to be at home is loosened and one by one they slink away. Mammy's heart sinks at the thought.

Often it begins when one child leaves early. It starts with a phone call.

> 'SAVAGE! And when are ye heading down … tomorrow? … Haha, legends … Haha. Yeah, doing my nut here … Yeah, bit of cabin fever … Yeah I. Just. Can't. Eat. Another. Quality. Street. Haha … Yeah … OK … later … bbbbbbbye.'

He hangs up, all excited, as if this is his golden ticket out of here. Mammy wants to know more.

'Who was that?'

'Just one of the lads. They're all going down to Lahinch tomorrow. They've a house there.'

'Lahinch.'

'Yeah ... it's great craic this time of year ... Surfing and the whole lot.'

'Surfing.'

'So I was thinking ... I might go down ... you know, see what the banter is ...'

'Banter.'*

'Yeah ... the craic ...'

'You've hardly been home a few hours and you're thinking of going away again already?'

'I'll be down again in a few weeks.'

This is a lie; once safely back within the zone of banter, Young Lad will be fully occupied, presumably with further bantering.

---

*The word 'banter' originated in the seventeenth century, and meant good-humoured teasing. It now describes virtually any human activity where there are a group of lads and some sort of verbal interaction between them. The word was so hated by Jonathan Swift that in 1710 he wrote an article denouncing it.

'And who else is going on this … Excursion?'

Mammy pronounces the word 'excursion' as if implying the event will feature in next year's *Rough Guide to Orgies and Other Carry-On*.

'Just the lads from work.'

'But you'll see them at work.'

Young Lad sighs. How can he explain to Mammy that seeing people at work is one thing but spending a couple of nights having 'the bantz'** (and possibly the lulz***) is a completely different story? Plus, Ciara will be there.

Mammy realizes she's lost this argument as Mammies have lost the 'Can't you stay here' argument all through the history of socializing.

'Go on so. I suppose you'll be wanting a lift?'

'No, Niall's picking me up here.'

'I see.'

What Mammy sees is a child straining to get away, and now that he's being collected up at the house, she won't even have the chance to have a one-on-

---

** 'Bantz' is an abbreviation of banter which is increasing in usage. In any civil society, it would be outlawed on pain of a thrashing with willow rods, but is strangely acceptable in Ireland. It's likely it would have given Jonathan Swift an aneurism.

*** Don't even ask.

one with him about his gallivanting levels. Mammy knows she has to cram as much guilt into her next statement as possible.

'I thought you might have liked to stick around this time, especially as your sister is only back from Australia for a short bit of time and we hardly see you at all. And you were only saying before Christmas that you were looking forward to the rest and there you are going off 'partying' again but I suppose if you want to spend time with your friends then you might as well. We'll amuse ourselves here, no doubt. We're used to it. Although what we're going to do with all the food in the house I don't know …'

Young Lad looks down at himself as if watching his resolve ebb away.

'I could go down a day later, I suppose.'

'Of course you could and you could have a bit more time here with your family.'

'Yeah, I suppose.'

'And shur what's going to happen there without you?'

A lot, as it turned out:

Air Pain

This is only half the story, of course. The nearby children only get it in the neck because they can come and go by land or short-haul aircraft, but there's no messing with longer journeys. It would be sad to see them go but Mammy wouldn't countenance the expense of changing flights.

The airport after Christmas is miserable. There are no banners or balloons. Just drained expressions and blear. The night before might have been a heavy one and the double whammy of booze blues and goodbyes is hitting at the same time. Mammies are trying to fill some of the in-between time with Haveyougotyours — 'Passports?' 'Yes,

Mammy.' 'Tickets?' 'I checked in online, Mammy, and I have my boarding pass.' 'Keys? You'd be awful stuck without them.' 'Yes, Mammy.'

But there's no delaying the inevitable. In contrast to ten days ago when the family watched the arrivals screen with anticipation, now they stare up at a grim reality.

DEPARTURES ✈		11:45
TIME	DESTINATION	REMARKS
TOO SOON	Australia	No work at home and some of them fellas in the Dáil with three pensions.
TOO SOON	New Zealand	It's not as far as it used to be I suppose. Although it's far enough.
TOO SOON	Canada	Minus FIFTY it is there now. Celsius or Fahrenheit, I can't remember which.
TOO SOON	D'bai	What. Ever. You. Do. I says to her, stay out of trouble Out There.
TOO SOON	Kazakhstan or is it the other one?	He says he'll come home when he has his money made. He'd better. You wouldn't know what Putin'd do.
TOO SOON	South Africa	You hear such awful stories, you know.
TOO SOON	Hamburg	He brought a lovely girl home to meet us. Anka was her name. I hope she'll put manners on him.
TOO SOON	Brussels	'Tis a cushy enough number she has out there. Some sort of EU thing.
NOT SOON ENOUGH	Home, wherever that is	We said to them to call in if they were ever in Ireland, as you do, but we didn't think they'd be here for CHRISTMAS. None of them had any English and poor Paddy didn't know what to do with them. And he's Not Well, you know.

Off into the miserable grey January sky they go.

Cat and House

No matter what the method of goodbye, Puss doesn't care. By January 6th, Puss has had enough. These people have been 'all up in Puss's grill' for too long. It's not just the endless photos of Puss just being Puss (WHY DO THEY FIND IT SO FASCINATING?), but they were always 'there', leaving doors open, sitting on Puss's chair, making Mammy stressed with their presence. And when Mammy is stressed, she forgets things. Things like the Importance of Puss.

The departure of the interlopers is a return to business as usual for Puss. The dog, of course, takes everything at face value.

Mammy is facing into the prospect of the rest of the long winter with an emptier house.

'Women's Christmas my foot,' she thinks.

THE END

Except it's not the end …

New Year, New Mammy

I'm not going to let it get to me

Life must go on, even in January. It's not easy. The house is in a state. Bits of wrapping paper keep turning up from underneath the couch along with the plastic gimmicks from the crackers. The remains of the Christmas cake have been frozen to be taken out as a surprise in June. The tree has been dragged, kicking and shedding, out of the house. Even the embryonic 'stretch in the evenings'* is cold comfort.

---

* One day, shortly after Christmas, a Mammy will go for her walk, look up at the sky, check her watch and announce: 'Do you know something? I think there's a bit of a stretch in the evenings.'

A 'bit of a stretch' has few benefits. It only serves to cast some light on how bad the weather is.

A mighty stretch — this is the king of stretches. It starts around May. A mania takes hold of the population. In the leafier suburbs, tag rugby starts up and the parks are alive with the sounds of competitive men and women shouting at team-mates who 'only joined up for the social aspect'. In the countryside fifteen-year-olds start tearing around the place in monstrous tractors drawing silage and leaving a trail of destroyed gateposts behind them.

Ould lads are 'tipping away', the euphemism for the kind of unplanned work where one thing leads to another and before long they are halfway through a major construction project just as it gets dark. They had intended to just whitewash a pillar but with the grand evening that was there, they could have a dry stone wall built up a mountain.

The optimism can't last too long. Once 21 June passes you are technically within your rights to announce: 'Ah, the days are KNACKERED now.'

And after that, all there is to look forward to is Christmas.

The atmosphere in Mammy's workplace doesn't help. A box of Roses on the empty desk just has a few Coffee Escapes and The Strawberry One left over. Otherwise it mostly contains empty wrappers. Tommy, on a ladder, unhooks the decorations from the ceiling tiles. Everywhere there are reminders of what time of year it is, and isn't.

'Your Out of Office is still on, Cat!'

'Oh, wishful thinking, haha!'

But out of the ashes there is new growth. It soon becomes clear that one of the altercations at the Christmas party has become official.

Dee from HR is in a Relationship with **Dylan the lunatic**

Orla Grogan WTF GIRL?!!! How come I miss all the goss. Haha. Phone call and details please !!!!

Office Mammy Very happy for you two. I have a lovely photo of the pair of ye from the Christmas do

Paul Ledgebag I've photos too! #Kardashian.

Dee From HR Stay classy Paul. #clown

This causes a bit of awkwardness as there was a full and frank exchange of views following the initial incident. Now that it's official, several of the lads realize some of the opinions they expressed constitute slagging off someone else's girlfriend.

But other than that, January is about penance. The wages of sin are diets. The canteen is full of lunches brought in and Tupperware that still has the faint hue of October's bolognese. Snatches of conversation revolve around excess, punishment, redemption and hope.

> 'Cooked a big pot of them last night. The house still smells of them …'

> '… Supposed to be low GI.'

> '… Antioxidants …'

> 'Supposed to speed up your metabolism …'

> 'Chia seeds? I thought that was the car with the seven-year warranty. Haha.'

> 'Shut up, Barry …'

> '… And how is it different to the normal juicer?'

> 'You could throw anything into it. We had a dose of kale yesterday.'

> 'Kale? We used to give that to cattle.'

'They're all eating it in New York now.'

'And they have fierce swanky cattle in New York ...'

'I just knock it back without thinking too much about it, to tell you the truth.'

'Looks like a sample you'd bring to the doctor.'

'C'MON, BARRY, I'm trying to eat!'

'Oprah swears by it. It's in the *O* magazine. I have it here in my bag. Where is it now — here it is: *Shine a light on a brand new you. You will FEEL the difference.* The only difference I notice is that I'm bound up like a mummy. But they say to stick at it for two weeks ...'

'Does it have a pool?'

'No, it's a Ben Dunne ...'

'Quinoa.'

'You mean Keenwah.'

'Oh, is that how you say it? Anyway it's one of these superfoods. Th'Incas were stone mad for it.'

'For all the good it did them.'

It's an orgy of self-examination. There's talk of Zumba, Pilates, Bokwa. Mammy's not one for classes but she's not immune to the relentless barrage of guilt-tripping that seems to be facing her whichever way she looks.

Mammy
likes a page
Rock Hard Abs For Mammies

Day 1	Day 12

Mammies! There's nothing at all wrong with ye. But if ye DID feel inclined to lose a bit here or there, our 12-day programme wouldn't do ye any harm at all.

Not that ye need to at all.

Only if ye thought ye did.

I. Won't. Say. Another. Word. About. It.

Himself is no help with the workout.

And, of course, like a lot of Mammies, one of her Christmas presents was a book about the Latest Thing Now: Mindfulness.

She might as well give the CD that came with it a go:

> *C'mere to me, I want to talk to ye. Mammies are
> FEROCIOUS for living in the past and the future.
> We worry about what so-and-so meant by that;
> where we're going to get the money for this; why
> that child decides to draw on the wall with I-don't-
> even-want-to-say; how in the name of God she
> ended up meeting that 'yoke' and she a grand girl.
> And this is in addition to all we've to do at work
> especially as 'this new one' isn't pulling her weight
> at all but if you say anything of course ... well you
> can't. Isn't she a niece of the boss?*

> *Enough! Mammies – it's time to start thinking of
> the present.*

'She has a point,' thinks Mammy. 'Although that
reminds me – I need to get something for one of
the girls in the office who's getting married next
week.'

> *The first thing is preparation. Get them all out of
> the house. They'll be fine. Turn off Joe Duffy. It'll
> only depress you. Sit down. Are you comfortable?
> Take off that scarf. You don't need it at all.
> Now are you still there? Right. Step one. Give
> a good big breath in. That's the girl. As you're
> breathing in, identify your in-breath as the in-breath
> and the out-breath as the out-breath.*

'This is my in-breath.'

'Meow.'

'Ah go away, Puss. Can I not get five minutes? I'll feed you in a minute. Pheewwww — this is my out-breath.'

'Meow.'

Now, step two: follow your in-breath from beginning to end for three-to-four seconds. Make sure your mind is always with it. Don't be distracted. Just think of nothing else but your breath all the way to the end. Your awareness is sustained. There is no interruption.

Bip-Bip-Bip-Bip Beeeep-Beeep Bip-Bip-Bip

'Ah, MAM!'

The third step is to grow in your awareness of your body as you are breathing. Say to yourself, 'I know my body is there. Mind and body is there.'

'I know my bo—'

'Anybody home?'

The oil-man is shouting in the door. They have to get a fill. How much is this going to cost? By the time she sorts that out, Himself is back.

The fourth step will help you achieve true mindfu—

'You're still at that Dalai Lama stuff.'

'IT'S MINDFULNESS. NAMEOFGOD CAN I NOT GET SOME BIT OF TIME TO MYSELF TO MEDITATE?!'

But then, just when her resolve is weakening:

234

The next time Himself arrives in, Mammy is far more relaxed.

And so with her feet deservedly up, we leave Mammy once again. Just don't forget to ring to say you arrived safely.

Acknowledgements

Thanks firstly to Brian and Eoin, my publishers at Transworld. Aside from 'giving me the bit of work' and all the editing, they were encouraging and helpful in teasing out the little nuggets that make an Irish Christmas — and especially an Irish Mammy Christmas — worth writing about. Thanks also to Katrina, Phil, Vivien, Richard and all at Transworld for their help during the crucial 'turn this thing into a book' stage. Thanks again to Faith at Lisa Richards Agency for all the practical advice and support.

Thanks to Doug Ferris who has once again turned my scrawls-on-a-wall into the warm and witty illustrations throughout the book. Thanks also to Peter O'Sullivan for help with additional illustrations.

Thanks and love to my multi-talented wife Marie for: ideas, suggestions, illustrations, edits, encouragement, and laying out the actual book.

Thanks to Mama* and Dada who have always been supportive and laid back — the perfect combination.

Thanks to the more than 140,000 Twitter followers of @irishmammies. For nearly three years, their contributions have been a joy to read as they relate their own fond observations of this Irish institution. Thanks for tagging along!

---

* You would think I would call her Mammy, wouldn't you, but I've been living a lie all these years.

About the Author

Colm O'Regan is a critically acclaimed stand-up comedian, columnist and broadcaster.

He writes a weekly column for the *Irish Examiner* and has written for *The Irish Times* and *BBC Online Magazine*. Colm is a regular contributor on Irish radio and on the BBC World Service. As a stand-up comedian, he has performed to sell-out crowds all over the world from Tokyo to Cape Town and including the Edinburgh Fringe, the Cat Laughs and the Montreal Just For Laughs Festival. His stand-up has also featured on RTÉ's *Late Late Show* and on Comedy Central. Colm also set up and runs the @irishmammies Twitter account which is where this whole thing started. It's followed by over 140,000 people and is still going strong.

This is his third book. The first two — *Isn't It Well For Ye?* and *That's More Of It Now* — have been nipping in and out of the bestseller lists since their publication. From Dripsey in County Cork, Colm now lives in Dublin but is always keen to get the news from home.

Also by Colm O'Regan

Isn't It Well For Ye?

the book of Irish Mammies

Explore the phenomenon of the Irish Mammy and what she might say about everything from the 'new mass' to the cardinal sin of not owning a cough bottle and the importance of airing clothes properly.

So if you're an Irish Mammy, have one, know one or suspect you might be turning into one, this book will act as your guide.

Shortlisted for Best Irish Published Book of the Year at the Irish Book Awards

'A hilarious analysis of the woman in all our lives … It deserves an award just for the title'

Irish Independent

'Isn't he very smart now?
If he was half as smart at his exams …'

Irish Mammy Magazine

Also by Colm O'Regan

That's More Of It Now

the second book of Irish Mammies

That's More Of It Now takes us even deeper into this parallel universe, with advice on everything from how to tell Mammy she is about to become a Granny to how to discipline a child (aged 0-45). Enjoy popular fairy-tales retold with an Irish Mammy at the centre of them; marvel at exclusive, not-yet-released scenes from the epic *Game of Scones*; and find some essential apps for the Modern Mammy's tablet.

Probably the most important sequel since *The Godfather Part II*, or at least *Fifty Shades Darker*, *That's More Of It Now* will change the way you see the world. Or at least make you laugh into your tea.

'Hilarious and moving tome from
one of our leading comics'

Hot Press Magazine*

---

* No honestly, this is the name of an Irish music and culture magazine, in case you think it had been reviewed by Mammy's second favourite publication.